More Praise foi

"There is no better guide—or collaborative partner—
for navigating the moral territory of post-traumatic living
than Larry Graham. In *Moral Injury: Restoring Wounded
Souls,* Graham sounds a clarion call for religious leaders
to cultivate habits of mind and body to meet the complex
situations of our day. Rather than offering a birds-eye
view of the moral terrain, Graham invites readers to feel
the earth under their feet and attune themselves to the
climate of their moral environments. With his careful def-
initional work and theological acumen, he revivifies theological ethics for progressive Christians. And beyond this
audience, Graham displays the importance of theology in
contemporary discussions of moral injury."
—Shelly Rambo, Associate Professor of Theology,
Boston University School of Theology, Boston, MA

"Graham gives us a remarkably wise and timely resource. Not only does he deepen conceptions of moral injury in the context of war, he also recasts the concept as
a rich, constructive resource for the daily work of pastors
who accompany parishioners in moral reflection and efforts to heal the wounds of moral dilemmas that comprise
contemporary life."
—Nancy J. Ramsay, Professor of Pastoral Theology
and Pastoral Care, Brite Divinity School,
Fort Worth, TX

Larry Kent Graham

Moral Injury

Restoring Wounded Souls

Abingdon Press

Nashville

MORAL INJURY:
RESTORING WOUNDED SOULS

Copyright© 2017 by Abingdon Press

All rights reserved.

Library of Congress Cataloging-in-Publication Data has been requested.

ISBN 978-1-5018-0075-7

Unless otherwise indicated, all Scripture quotations are from the Common English Bible. Copyright © 2011 by the Common English Bible. All rights reserved. Used by permission. www.CommonEnglish Bible.com.

The poem on page 141 is used by permission of the author and translator. Nijaz Alispahic, "Nadrastanje Boli [Overgrowth of Pain]" in Karakazan. Radio Kameleon Tuzla, Bosanska Biblioteka Klagenfurt/ Celovec-Austria, Lojze Weiser: 1996. Translated text "Overcoming Pain," as printed here, was communicated to the author in an interview with the translator, who prefers to remain anonymous.

Portions of chapter 10 are adapted from previous articles written by the author and published in the following journals:

Larry Kent Graham, "Political Dimensions of Pastoral Care in Community Disaster Response," *Journal of Pastoral Psychology* 63, no. 4 (2014): 471–88. With permission of Springer.

Larry Kent Graham, "Pastoral Theology and Catastrophic Disaster," *Journal of Pastoral Theology* 16, no. 2 (Fall 2006): 1–17.

17 18 19 20 21 22 23 24 25 26—10 9 8 7 6 5 4 3 2 1
MANUFACTURED IN THE UNITED STATES OF AMERICA

To Sheila Greeve Davaney
Always True North

Contents

Acknowledgments

This book is about collaborative creativity in addressing complex moral challenges. It would not have been written without the collaborative generosity of way too many people to name here. But a few stand out. Kathy Armistead, formerly of Abingdon Press, gets all the credit for recruiting me to take on this project. She defeated my many refusals and objections. Bruce Fenner of the General Board of Higher Education and Ministry ensured that I would have a place to try out these ideas with United Methodist clergy endorsed for specialized ministry. He also agreed to help fund the production of this book as a service to the church as well as to the endorsed community. When David Teel became my editor, his deft touch, personal support, and understanding of my capacity for detour ensured that the book would not only be completed, but useful. I thank Katherine Johnston and her production team for their excellent guidance and detailed attention.

Numerous clergy colleagues added their insights. The Endorsed Community of the United Methodist Church spent many hours in my workshops, testing the promise and limits of collaborative conversation. I am especially appreciative that several ecclesiastical leaders and parish-based clergy agreed to comprise a focus group to identify moral concerns and identify promising ways to respond. Rev. Dr. Valerie Jackson, Rev. Olon Lindemood, Rev. Stephanie Price, Rev. Dr. Vern Rempel, Rev. Dr. Melanie Rosa, and Rev. Dr. Eric Smith were astute, funny, and wise in their engagement with me and one another. From all of these clergy colleagues I learned again that "I am as we are!"

My pastor, George Anastos, provided pastoral care through a health crisis during the writing of this book, and perceptive insights about the various "micro-moral" decisions impinging on clergy moment by moment in ministry. Rev. Tracey Dawson offered counsel on issues in parish-based ministry, and Mary Martin illuminated the power of collaborative therapy and soul language in helping people heal from moral injury. Dorcia Johnson, a student assistant, gave the best reading imaginable on a floundering early draft of the proposal for this book. Participation with Dr. Rita Nakashima Brock, director of the Soul Repair Center, and Professor Nancy Ramsay, director of the Soul Repair think tank at Brite Divinity School were of inestimable value. My friend and colleague Professor Carrie Doehring of Iliff School of Theology was always available with resources, ideas, curiosity, and encouragement. Her work on trauma and moral stress are at the cutting edge. Professor Dana W. Wilbanks was a constant conversation partner, offering support and keen challenge at many points. Professor Miguel De La Torre, Rev. Bonita Bock, Pastor Joe Johnson, and Rev. Nadyne Guzman helped me link microsystemic and macrosystemic factors in responding to moral dissonance and resolving moral dilemmas. Chaplain Paul Dodd, US Army, retired; Tom Carpenter, Esq., of the Forum on the Military Chaplaincy; and Professor Shelly Rambo of Boston University were conversation partners in the context of our planning a consultation on Pathways to the Military Chaplaincy held in Boston in April 2015. Their extensive experience of addressing moral challenges and healing moral injuries informed much of what I have come up with.

I am immensely grateful for the eager interest that my children and family have taken in this book. One daughter was an editorial writer for a newspaper and is now a director of communications; another daughter is an English teacher. My son ingests ideas. My daughter-in-law works in communications and marketing. A third daughter visualizes ideas in color. All of them love to argue. The conversations were always collaborative. I listened to them with appreciation.

Finally, I have dedicated this book to Sheila Greeve Davaney, my life partner and the Harvey H. Potthoff Professor of Theology, Emerita, at Iliff School of Theology. There is no adequate way to convey Sheila's contributions. I can only state the most efficacious: encourager, advocate, prod, critic, editor, thought-leader, muse, bystander, reality-test, and guide. If this book passed muster with Sheila, there is some hope for the reader too.

Our Morally Saturated World

This book offers collaborative strategies to help ministers and those they serve to engage moral challenges. It assists them to discern the right thing to do in the face of moral dissonances and dilemmas. It also guides care in the difficult process of healing from moral injuries resulting from one's own actions as well as from the actions of others.

Moral injury is the erosive diminishment of our souls because our moral actions and the actions of others against us sometimes have harmful outcomes. It rises from our attempts to do the right thing as individuals and communities. Moral injury is personal, interpersonal, and collective. None of us escapes moral injury. We all bear the costs of attempted goodness.

We are keenly aware that to live morally is a perilous task. We all carry moral wounds deep in our souls. We have all failed to live up to our professed moral values. When our efforts to do the right thing fall short or have unintended consequences we can become frustrated and fractured by our efforts, leading to a sense of failure and futility. We have all harmed others by our actions and by our failure to act. We have been hurt by the righteousness of others as well as by blatantly immoral acts perpetrated upon us. Each of us is both a source and victim of moral injury to ourselves and others.

As moral creatures, each of us is continually faced with moral challenges. None of us is a moral island unto ourselves. And the moral qualities of our lives and the lives of others are not lost on us. It is estimated that about two-thirds of human conversation focuses on our opinions about the behaviors of others.[1] We are in continual inner dialogue about how well we are doing and what we think is good and bad in what others do or fail to do. We are gossipers, commentators, moral actors, recipients of the moral actions of others, and full of unending evaluations of what should and should not be going on. Our brains are live-streaming Op-Ed pages.

The needles on our moral compasses frequently point in different directions. Discovering our moral True North and following its course may clash with the True North on the moral compasses of our companions on the moral journey. We may enter disputed moral territory with various claims about how life will be arranged in these spaces. We argue a lot as individuals and community about what the right thing is, morally speaking. Contending values, moral dissonance, and injuries from moral disputes are rampant and unavoidable.

Naming these moral dynamics clearly will help us to understand and respect what is most sacred to one another. Knowing what is at stake in moral conflicts enables us to frame strategic responses by which to work toward positive outcomes, or to restrain harm. Strategic engagement, derived from collaborative framing of interests and options, can lead to more loving, just, and vital moral outcomes. The process of naming, framing, enacting, and revising our moral conundrums is the stuff of everyday moral dissonance, moral dilemmas, and healing from moral injury. They are the four pillars of healing and resilience in moral living.

This book, therefore, enters the messy, costly, and sometimes gratifying world of moral dissonance, dilemma, injury, and healing. It is a practical book that tracks us through the morasses and advances of daily living from a moral standpoint. It does not flinch at the difficulty. I recognize that much of our lives consist of accumulated moral stress. We carry a sense that we are slogging through multiple moral morasses with no clear path to moral high ground. It can be paralyzing to be overwhelmed by moral challenges. It can be wearying to our souls to accommodate the burdens of moral failure and moral injury. This book maps moral challenges and offers strategies for healing and resiliency when things go bad, morally speaking.

The pages that follow profess to bring clarity, healing, and guidance in the face of the many moral challenges and the ongoing wounds arising from our attempts as persons and communities to do the right thing. They seek to answer several critical questions woven into our attempts to be responsible moral agents.

- How do I understand myself as a moral being?

- How do I find assistance and moral guidance to sort through the pervasive (and often contradictory) moral claims upon me and mine?

- What engenders moral courage in me?

- How do I close the moral gap between my own values and the dominant values organizing my larger communities such as church, nation, and the world?

- What helps me to bear the pain of moral injury inflicted on me?

- Is there a safe place for me to heal from the injury caused to myself by the harm I have done to others?

- Is forgiveness possible?

- How am I to be restored and set free to do better?

Addressing these questions does not require bringing the reader to the author's own moral or ethical standpoint about the specific ethical issues of our time. Our moral landscape is thoroughly polarized. Moral signposts don't lead us to the same destination. In most cases, the capacity to fashion a common moral center is out of reach in the multiplicity of claims and counterclaims. As morally advanced and morally astute as the author may be, it would be foolhardy to suppose that one book or one point of view would coalesce all these compelling differences into a common, unified moral sentiment.

This book is about moral betterment in the face of moral dissonance. It is a practical guide that promotes healing, guidance, reconciliation, and various forms of moral advances in the personal and social circumstances of clergy and those they serve. The basic assumption of this writing is that the Christian call to love our neighbor as we love ourselves is a common call for clergy and laity. Clergy and laity need each other to discover ways to embrace moral dissonance and to turn moral challenges into spiritual advances for individuals and our large social networks. Doing the right thing together is a source of strength and vitality; it brings a sense of grace and gratitude to our lives. It is a source of blessing. Sharing our moral challenges helps us meet them; sharing our moral burdens helps us bear them. Embracing one another when moral failures wound and trap us is part of the call to make one another whole through shared remorse, repentance, forgiveness, and reconciliation.

In my view, the core issue of North American Christianity today is not to find an overarching moral center or a common moral stance on the many complex issues we face. Rather, the core issue of our time is how to embrace with grace and care the dissonance and diverse assessments of the moral issues calling for our guidance and healing. To bring our strengths and moral energies to bear in today's fragmented moral climate, I believe that we need to become more astute about the intractable differences that separate us. We need to become more productively engaged with those with whom we disagree. Above all, we need greater facility in being accountable for the injuries that we inflict. We would benefit from mutual assistance in bearing the depletion of our souls resulting from trying to do the right thing and be a good person in the face of overwhelming moral complexities. We need better skills at loving our moral enemies. We need moral flexibility and productive collaboration. We need to better access modes of healing and resiliency in the moral arena.

In short, this book is a guide to help pastors, parishioners, and religious organizations to do better with everyday moral challenges and to heal from wounds to the souls of persons and communities arising from one another's actions. Simply put, we are inescapably moral, pervasively wounding, and inevitably wounded.

Within this sea of moral dissonance, fatigue, and injury, are there ways to find and sustain a lively engagement? Can we find a way to address our moral differences and to do the right thing in such a manner that does not impair the grace, love, and justice that give rise to our aspirations in the first place? Can we handle moral challenges without creating moral injury? I am confident that the answer to these questions is an affirmative yes.

Part I

Mapping the Moral Landscape

CHAPTER 1

Setting Our Course

Judging a Book by Its Cover

The title of the book and the cover image of a shattered compass can be read in at least three ways. The most common reading is that individuals and communities have accurate moral compasses but they have become broken through life events and life choices. We need to repair the compass. And this book will certainly be helpful to those who have broken their compasses and lost their way.

There is a second equally important reading of the cover. The second reading implies that our moral compasses need to be broken if we are going to heal and find the right path for ourselves and our communities. Our souls and the souls of our communities are injured because we rely on faulty compasses to guide us. To repair wounded or misdirected souls sometimes means that we need to break and remake our moral orientation, or at least reset our moral compasses. When the rich young ruler asked Jesus what he had to do to be saved, Jesus broke the young man's compass and offered another: "Go, sell what you own, and give the money to the poor."[1]

Third, the cover could be read as though moral compasses and wounded souls are references to individuals, and that there is only one moral compass to worry about. Such a reading could not be more wrong. Moral compasses are given to us by our communities and cultures. They arise within our souls from our past histories and our present contexts. They always establish us at a place in time and history and point our journeys into territories inhabited by other people. The people traveling toward or with us are sometimes friends, companions, families, and associates. The individuals and social groups we encounter are sometimes strangers, competitors, rivals, and even enemies. They have moral compasses too. We continually struggle to identify the compasses we need to read the moral dissonances that arise as we travel through a peopled world. We constantly need to reset our compasses to take us toward healing of the injuries that have been inflicted upon us as well as those we have brought about because our compasses have been set wrong or we did not follow them. And we need compasses to help us track through a world of people and groups following compasses that may not point in the same directions that we are obligated to travel.

The core idea of this book is that healing soul wounds arising from moral injuries requires sophisticated and courageous embracing of our moral pain, and the pain of changing our moral compasses and moral directions as required by the actual circumstances of our lives. The moral challenges we face are here to stay. We should welcome them because, though difficult, they provide occasions to engage one another in collaborative processes by which we might create healthy alternatives within the moral landscapes we inhabit. This book proffers specific strategies to help ministers and laypersons be clearer about our moral centers, the True North of our moral compasses. It provides guidance for more productively handling the irresolvable moral conflicts between us, and for contributing to the moral betterment of our social communities. The book offers assistance for understanding and healing the moral injuries we inflict and receive as we move in varying directions across the moral territories of our lives.

Starting Points

There are five dominant influences on my decision to enter the morass of moral conflict, moral injury, and resilience. They illuminate why I became a guide in this territory. The maps and compasses I recommend derive from a complex array of factors.

First, my work as a professor, caregiver, and writer in the field of pastoral theology and care exposed me to a number of contending moral values in my own ministry and the case studies presented for consultation. In my theorizing about the person-world relationship constructing our ministries of care, I realized that contending moral values are an ineluctable part of our existence. One simply cannot teach and practice pastoral care without facility in recognizing and helping others to address moral issues.

Second, my research and teaching specifically on the impact of war on family pastoral care led to an awareness of the pervasiveness of trauma, moral injury, and the power of healing soul wounds through collaboration, truth-telling, forgiveness, and reconciliation. I interviewed families in the United States, Germany, Bosnia and Herzegovina, and Vietnam about their experiences of war in order to find out more about the moral ambiguities of fighting wars and rebuilding family lives after war. In all cases, moral dissonance, moral dilemmas, and moral injuries were front and center in their narratives. I learned from families around the world the powerful ways that forgiveness, lamentation, and community solidarity sustained them in the face of war's cruelties and empowered their recovery.

Third, my colleague Carrie Doehring and I accepted an invitation from the United States Air Force to establish a new Master of Arts in Military PTSD for active duty Air Force chaplains. We worked with six Air Force chaplains over a three-year period on resiliency training and healing from the wounds of war. Following this, Dr. Doehring and I participated in the Soul Repair think tank sponsored by the Soul Repair Center at Brite Divinity School. The Soul Repair Center has become a leading national resource in research, treatment, and education related to healing moral injury in the wounded souls of veterans and their families. Much of the work in this book derives from my participation in these programs and my collaboration with Professor Doehring and colleagues in the Soul Repair think tank.

Fourth, during 2015, I coordinated workshops with the endorsed community of United Methodist specialized ministers and conducted focus-group conversations with parish-related ministers on healthy living in the face of moral dissonance. Working with about two hundred military, hospice, and healthcare chaplains, pastoral counselors, life-coaches, parish ministers, and police chaplains made me realize that moral injury can accrue from accumulated stress in morally dissonant environments as much as from failure to act in accordance with one's own moral codes. Parish ministers and ecclesiastical leaders responsible for the moral vitality of their churches report soul-numbing stressors from the conflicts inherent at all levels in their work, and in the discordant moral visions at work in their denominations. I draw on their experiences to illustrate how moral dissonance, dilemmas, and injuries might be positively used in addressing moral challenges.

I also write from the standpoint of a married, heterosexual, white, male, financially secure, North American liberal, and progressive Protestant Christian. I am a retired theological professor and a senior citizen, born during World War II and coming into my core adult moral narratives during the Vietnam War, and the Civil Rights, gay, and feminist liberation movements of the 1960s and 1970s. I am a brother, uncle, husband, father, grandfather, and great-grandfather. I address or assume an audience of Protestant Christians, but I also seek to write with a nonsectarian pluralistic public theological accent. This writing may prove to be inadequately Christian for some readers and too infused by Christian moral themes for others. But I hope that the engagement with what is presented here will help readers clarify the moral mirrors into which they gaze and to help them see better what is there to see in themselves and around them.

Audiences

This book has three audiences. First, it is oriented toward ministers and religious leaders who, as moral human beings, face and struggle with the same moral dissonances, injuries, and conflicts as the rest of humanity. This book is not just to help ministers aid others but to engage their own struggles and wounding. We, as ministers, need to engage our own moral conundrums. There is truth in the ancient adage "physician heal yourself," though this book will give that old wisdom a decidedly social twist.

Second, the audience for the book is not just the minister as engaged in his or her own conflicts. It also seeks to aid ministers as they work with individuals and communities around moral conflicts. Thus the audience is also ministers who are moral healers and guides. The point of this book is that ministers cannot be adequate moral healers and guides without also engaging the conflicts and stresses of their own moral worlds.

A third audience is laypersons. All of us are moral beings and all of us need to consider our moral situations and find better and more creative processes for navigating the tensions, conflicts, and choices that continually present themselves. There is no opting out for humans having to participate in our interconnected world.

Collage

This writing covers a broad moral landscape. The ethical and value options are beyond enumeration. I do not enter this landscape with a single moral or ethical standpoint that presumes to lead the reader to a moral advance on any particular moral dilemma or conflict compelling our response. I do not presume to regard myself as a moral exemplar of any or all of the issues I take up in this writing. What I attempt is to portray a variety of approaches to naming, framing, enacting, and revising the moral dissonances we face, as well as reenacting the moral dilemmas and injuries in our concrete lives through a variety of tools. I will draw on theology, ethics, psychology, pastoral and spiritual care, journalistic investigation, editorial analyses, personal autobiography, pastoral case studies, and various literary traditions to understand, engage, and advance moral options in concrete or everyday circumstances. Informal conversations, pastoral anecdotes, and web-based discourse will be woven into the conversation.

The presentation of this book will be circular rather than linear, kaleidoscopic instead of monocular, collaborative rather than individualistic, embodied rather than principled. It will be messy and edgy, but not incoherent. Rather than a painting, I offer you a pastiche: a collage of moral engagements fashioned from the materials we find in our everyday living that shape our moral standpoints and provide tools for our moral responses. But I do offer what I believe are some very important and useful ways of enacting our moral dissonances, dilemmas, and energies as responsible, resilient, and morally concerned individuals and communities.

As you can tell from the Contents, this book is not a linear work; it is circular and redundant, like most of our thoughts and actions. You can start almost anywhere and read forward or backward from there. Themes, examples, and methods of engaging moral challenges do build on one another. You may read the book through from the beginning with a positive cumulative effect. Or you can read each topic, strategic example, and habits-of-mind exercise as a standalone entry. In postmodern terms, this is an exercise in multi-partiality. In the words of the main character in Don DeLillo's short story "Sine, Tangent, Cosine," "Ordinary moments make the life.... I inhale the little drizzly details of the past, and know who I am. What I failed to know before is clearer now, filtered up through time, and experience belonging to no one else, not remotely, no one, anyone, ever."[2]

This book is about a way of life, not a point of view. I hope that my approach will bring color, richness, and vitality to your way of being in the world as a moral agent. I hope that there are a few passages in serious sections that make you laugh. I hope it empowers you to bear your moral burdens, heal your moral injuries, and forbear in love the moral failures of others. I invite you to read on to see what this might mean.

CHAPTER 2

Doing the Right Thing

The fabric of the moral life is woven from threads spun in our everyday interactions. We continually ask ourselves what is the right thing to do in our unique circumstances. Every inner dialogue that we have with ourselves, and every verbal and behavioral conversation that we have with others, is a social process infused with moral elements. We are moral beings through and through and can never shut off the moral turbines that idle and roar inside and around us.

When as Christians we commit to the moral obligation to love our neighbor as we love ourselves, we commit to standards of action that aim to result in morally positive outcomes such as healing, beauty, and justice.[1] Though the call to be intentionally engaged in receiving and giving beneficence to one another can be inconvenient and overwhelming, it is truly gratifying—and sometimes even exhilarating—to feel that we have done the right thing. In these circumstances we begin to sense the meaning of the aphorism that "it is more blessed to give than to receive." And, looking deeper, we begin to recognize that moral engagement is not only a matter of linear or one-directional giving and receiving, but a complex interaction and mutually enhancing process of simultaneously receiving through giving. Moral action is not so much an act of individual agency from one to another, but a complex social interactional mixture of engagement by people living in the same or intersecting moral matrices in which all parties are receivers and givers. Each is enhanced beyond what they give and receive because the goodness generated by the collaborative process of giving and receiving reflects the power of grace and the creativity of loving. Such giving and receiving spin a rich and enduring web of life that holds and nurtures us and all other living things.

Chapter 2

Healing, Sustaining, and Guiding

This book seeks to engage the Christian moral task from my perspective as a pastoral theologian, caregiver, and psychotherapist.[2] Pastoral theology combines caring and theologizing to develop both theory and advances in practices of care suitable for ministry and the common good. Its scope is personal, relational, social, communal, political, and cosmic.

The three dominant functions or aspects of pastoral theology, classically understood, have been healing, sustaining, and guiding.[3] To these have been added surviving, liberating, transforming, and envisioning.[4] I believe that this book's focus on moral guidance and healing from moral injury combines all of these aspects of pastoral theology in a coherent and usable manner.

Healing in the context of moral injury, as I will develop it, reorients persons toward the consequences of past harm perpetrated by them or upon them. Surviving egregious harm and trauma is a form of healing and sustaining life in the face of its negations. Liberating persons and groups to refashion their moral landscapes is itself a dimension of healing and moral engagement and requires guidance. Envisioning is a form of letting go of harmful moral codes and instituting new modes of personal and communal practices. Healing of past harm perpetrated and received comes into place by naming one's moral truths, reframing those truths in actionable terms, enacting moral alternatives, and revising one's moral engagement in the world in more vital terms.

The emphasis upon moral guidance that this book brings to pastoral theology and care will prove novel and challenging for some. Guiding has probably been the least appreciated—and the least developed—aspect of pastoral theology. Guiding was too closely associated with "advice-giving," "problem-solving," "authoritarianism," "mind control," "evangelization," "indoctrination," "moralizing," and "intellectualizing." The field of pastoral care has tended to regard moral concerns as moralistic and judgmental rather than an inherent part of pastoral care and counseling.[5]

However, more recently, pastoral theology has become newly oriented toward the moral dimensions of life. This development has built on the recognition of the intricate relationships and dynamics between individuals and their contexts. Accordingly, there has been an important push for pastoral theologians and caregivers to orient our theory and practices toward liberating and transforming the pervasive structures of intersecting oppressions of gender, sexual orientation, race, and class.[6]

In the last few years, two new types of moral concerns have come to the fore and have extended the more social and communal emphases in pastoral theology and care. These new concerns have emerged out of historical circumstances and changes in contemporary culture; they represent new issues emergent in our day.

Both are central to this book. The first is the challenge to value differences and engage them productively within and across religious and political groupings. Sometimes called "intercultural pastoral care," this range of moral concerns seeks to find non-hegemonic ways to respect and work creatively with the religiously infused conflicting political and social visions in our body-politic. The interplay of religious moral visions and political agendas in the church and nation in the United States cries out for healing and moral guidance at the personal, social, communal, and cultural levels.[7]

The second type of moral concern is the major focus of this book: the emergence of "moral injury" as a distinct dimension of spiritual care for post-traumatic healing. The term *moral injury* has come into more general parlance these past few years through greater awareness of the moral burdens of many war veterans. These burdens may not always be accessible to them or apparent to others. They sometimes are subsumed as an element of post-traumatic stress or post-traumatic stress disorder (PTS/PTSD). We have come to see, however, that moral stress and moral injury among combat veterans may not equate with or be subsumed totally under PTS or PTSD. The emergence of moral struggles may come later in life—decades later—and be unsettling for the veteran and others. In these circumstances, the sense of moral conflict, struggle, and even moral failure, comes into the foreground, requiring spiritual and religious attention along with psychological and therapeutic intervention.

But the concept is not limited, as we shall discover, to veterans. There are many ways that we all struggle with moral injury, when moral injury is broadly understood as the failure to live in accordance with our deepest moral aspirations and as the diminishment that comes from our own actions as well as the actions of those against us. Moral injury—both rendered and received—is a dominant challenge in our current environments. Indeed, we may say that the toxic moral climate in which we find ourselves is more than injurious. We may even discover that it will prove fatal.

How, then, do pastoral caregivers and religious communities employ a pastoral standpoint to bring moral guidance and promote healing from moral injury? I believe there are two foci to caregiving with persons and groups about moral challenges: sharing the risks and co-creative discovery. The link between these is attunement and mutual active listening.

First, the pastoral caregiver, like the "shepherd" from which the Christian caregiver's role is derived, shares the participatory locus of risk with those for whom the caregiver is responsible. The pastoral caregiver lives in perpetual "anxious solicitude,"[8] within all the vicissitudes we face together as humans and with those seeking our help. The pastoral caregiver stands within, not outside or above, the pangs and promises of those needing care and guidance. There is spiritual "skin in the game," when we walk as companions in the moral journeys we are invited to join. The nature of care and guidance is always dependent upon the dynamics and dimensions inherent in the actual situation faced by all the parties that requires care, healing, guidance, and change. In short, relational availability and the authentic use of self are the foundations of pastoral care in providing moral guidance and healing moral injury.

Second, the pastoral caregiver is particularly attentive to the contextual possibilities of the situation and not just to the handbooks that teach him or her about tending to those in our care. It is in the mutual attunement to the constricting and harmful dynamics that the way forward is discerned. In the felt experience of the concrete moral conundrums, in the "here and the now," there is usually a unique dimension requiring particular emotional attunement, naming, and response. The pastoral caregiver knows that the resolution to a moral challenge is not what the caregiver applies to the situation. Neither is the resolution solely up to what the morally conflicted parties finally choose. The pastoral and spiritual caregiver knows that the direction of change, healing, and moral advances arise from the insights generated by the authentic relationship between the care provider and the careseeker as both engage in a safe partnership to address the difficult challenges before them. From this anxious, committed, collaborative attunement arises the possibility of contextually creative healing and moral advance.

I indicated that pastoral theology is a theological discipline linked to the practices of healing, sustaining, and guiding. Making a judgment about what is better or worse, suitable or not, healing or wounding, in the practice of pastoral and spiritual care involves coming to theological conclusions. So, as the book proceeds, there will be occasion to venture new theological and moral insights emergent from the locally engaged practice of moral healing, guidance, and transformation.

Moral Dissonance, Dilemmas, and Injury

It makes little sense to discuss moral injury without first understanding moral dissonance and moral dilemmas. Moral dissonance and moral dilemmas are inseparably intertwined with one another and the foundation for moral health as well as moral injury. I will give a fuller interpretation in chapters 6 and 7 of moral dissonance, dilemmas, and injuries, but a brief portrayal of each and their relation to one another will be a helpful anchor point for what follows throughout the book.

But first, what do I mean by *moral* in this writing?

By *moral* I mean the sense of right, fairness, and/or obligation that I feel in the events of my everyday life, including the core values and virtues held by my communities about what constitutes the best way to live.

Moral dissonance refers to the recognition that my internal sense of right and wrong is unclear or in conflict. Moral dissonance is sometimes referred to as moral stress, but one can experience moral dissonance without stress. Moral dissonance without stress is simply moral difference, which might actually be an enhancer rather than a stressor.

But moral dissonance is not just about one's personal interior conflicts. Moral dissonance most often arises from the moral climate in which history and culture have embedded us. By *moral climate* I mean the matrix of operative moral values and demands arising from our intersecting moral environments, which place obligations upon me and my communities. Such moral codes are connected to our families, cultures, religions, nation, ethnicity, gender, race, economics, professional lives, and politics. They are both hidden and transparent, synchronous and dissonant, liberating and oppressing. We all live in such multiple moral landscapes. These multiple moral environments are the source of pervasive moral dissonance in our personal and social lives. They generate enormous inner conflict, as well as conflict with groups holding other moral commitments.

Moral dilemmas refer to the tension and struggles that arise in individuals and communities when the pervasive dissonances in our moral landscapes become a stressful conundrum. Moral dilemmas require us to choose and act against one moral good at the expense of another value we hold. There is no escaping a moral dilemma when it comes into play. It is a crisis that requires a response. There are various possible outcomes to the dilemma. The results may be a moral advance. Or they may lead to moral injury or moral demise.

Moral injury, sometimes referred to as moral trauma, is the burden of harm and the diminishment of vitality that arises in individuals and communities when we (or others) violate our moral compasses. I will say more below about moral compasses, but for now it is enough to say that our moral compasses refer to the internalized organization of our moral identity (ethics, values, and moral codes). Moral injury comes about when our lives and the lives of our social groups diverge from what we believe to be the best in ourselves, or when our moral actions lead to a diminishment of value for self and others. Moral injury also occurs when others violate us and impair our moral sensibilities about right and wrong.

There are two sources of moral injury: agential moral injury brought upon ourselves by our own agency, and receptive moral injury caused to us by the agency of others. Agential moral injury arises in the gap between our aspirations and the consequences of our actions. When we do the wrong thing, or fail to do the right thing, or when our actions lead to unintended harm, we feel diminished morally and carry some measure of burden as a consequence. This burden, often felt as shame and guilt, is what I mean by agential moral injury, even when we are unaware that it exists.

Receptive moral injury is the diminishment to our moral compasses and our sense of personal goodness that results from the actions of individuals and communities against us. Victims and survivors of sexual and domestic violence, for example, may have their moral compasses about life's goodness and their own sense of personal worth broken by what happened to them and the moral assessments they make of it. Or individuals and groups shattered by war, natural disasters, and other cataclysms may wonder if there is a good God running the show or if the universe is a trustworthy moral environment.

So, what is the relationship between moral dissonance, moral dilemmas, and moral injuries? While inevitable, moral conflicts and dissonance between moral values are not necessarily injurious. They may be frustrating and limiting. They may lead to misunderstanding and distance. But in themselves, they are part of the normal and even desirable fabric of human diversity. In fact, the creative interplay between dissonant moral options can lead to new syntheses and creative advances. Dissonance in moral living, as in music, may be resolved in wonderful ways. However, dissonances and dilemmas may also lead to moral injury if care is not taken. If moral dissonance and moral dilemmas are handled in a sensitive and productive manner, it is less likely that moral wounding will take place for self or others. And when moral dissonance and moral dilemmas are responded to with a measure of skill, there is a greater likelihood for moral healing and resilience to emerge.

This book is about how to negotiate moral dissonance and resolve moral dilemmas as means of preventing moral injury to self and others. It also guides the reader to various means of recovering from moral wounds in the souls of individuals and communities when they take place.

Two Leaky Metaphors

The notion of "moral injury" is a metaphor to describe a negative state of affairs in individuals and communities. It is very important to recognize that metaphors measure one set or range of experiences by terms more usually associated with another. "Injury" is a physical category and operates primarily in a healthcare context. "Moral" is a category of values, ethics, and laws, and operates in terms of actions, behaviors, and social conventions. "Moral" refers less to health and more to actions, behaviors, and social norms. It embraces the more or less rational and spiritual choices, aspirations, and meanings humans employ to live well. When mixing categories of experience, it is essential to recognize the gains from doing so. It is also important not to lose track of the differences and to what may be lost. Metaphors are evaluated both by what they include and by what they leave out.

The strength of the moral injury metaphor is that it is not moralistic, shaming, and condemning toward persons suffering from the pain of moral struggles and failings. It provides an affirming and safe locus to look deeply at what is going on and to find ways of moving to a richer and more vital relationship to the painful past. It recognizes our relative fragility and powerlessness over what happens to us, and over what we are sometimes forced to do in spite of our better judgment.

The notion of moral injury also points positively to the potential of a changed outcome: healing. The notion of healing implies that we are not destined to perpetual impairment based on the past but can join those powerful life forces dedicated to renewal, repair, and restoration. In short, removing stigmatizing and judgmental language about our moral actions lifts unnecessary burdens of conscience so that we might better heal and bear with strength the moral pain we are carrying.

The recent emergence of the language of "soul repair" and "moral injury" has in itself had healing effects. For example, one therapist reported that though her clients appreciate the language of PTSD and the language of current mental health treatment modes, "when the language and concepts of soul wound or soul injury are introduced, a place of substantial identity arises to consciousness in a profoundly tangible way." When they reframe "their suffering as a soul wound/injury, that deep inexplicable place in them of humanness becomes valid. By validating this reality, they can reclaim the experience of that deepest part of themselves and work on healing the wound." At the same time they "also honor the reality of the substantial place of identity... [and] they regain the experience of being human, connected to and valued as all other human beings." This is "a life changing shift in perception of self when the soul of the person becomes the focus of healing."[9]

In spite of these genuinely positive elements, there are, however, two downsides to the metaphor of moral injury. First, it is misleading about agency. Second, it medicalizes what is fundamentally an ethical and moral category.

Where should we locate moral agency or responsibility when assessing moral harm? Typically, agency is the responsibility of the actor and implies relative levels of choice. I am responsible for the harm I inflict on myself and others. Others are responsible for the harm they do to me. We presumably had other choices than to harm and be harmed, but in any case, the actor is responsible for his or her actions, whether intended to be harmful or not. Without accepting responsibility, the move toward healing, forgiveness, and reconciliation becomes extremely difficult. In fact, failure to assess and accept appropriate responsibility can increase and add greater complexity to the original injury.

However, when the metaphor "moral injury" is used, the locus of responsibility or agency becomes murky. In moral injury, three assessments must be made. First, we must discern who is responsible for the harmful action. Second, we must discern the harmful consequences of the actions both to the actor and to the recipients. Third, without blaming the victim, we also must assess how the recipient of the harmful actions may contribute to the harm by how they do or do not respond. The metaphor "moral injury" may make it difficult to distinguish these dimensions. We may blame the victim for how they respond, rather than assessing the moral actions of the perpetrator; or we may focus on the injury to the perpetrator rather than upon their moral actions. Recognizing that the agent of offense is also harmed by the offense—and that their harmful actions may be motivated by unresolved moral injuries in their own lives—may detour the focus to the perpetrator's injury and away from their harmful actions. Now the injuring party becomes the injured party. This changes the equation, and the focus of concern. When I am injured and impaired, compassion, empathy, and social support are relatively easy to come by. When my actions are morally offensive, rejection, punishment, and vilification are quick to follow. Compassion and nonjudgmental acceptance are much harder to come by. So, without care, the metaphor "moral injury" can, in itself, be utilized to avoid or diminish critically important dimensions of moral responsibility necessary for healing moral injury for both agents and receptors.

The other danger in the metaphor "moral injury" is that it medicalizes what is fundamentally a moral and ethical discourse. The strength of the healthcare context is that it is (1) non-moralistic, (2) (presumably) accessible to all, (3) treats without preconditions, (4) utilizes skilled personnel and technologies, and (5) is non-stigmatizing. The medical or healthcare environment is woven into the fabric of our culture and those needing its assistance are welcomed and treated with respect. We can expect no less for those struggling with the moral challenges of their lives and the devastation arising from moral dissonance, dilemmas, and injuries.

But, does the language frame of secular healthcare technologies give the best access to some potentially critical aspects of the moral dimensions of moral injury? Mary Martin, cited above, found that it helped her clients immensely to "de-medicalize" moral trauma by using the language of the soul. However, the metaphor of moral injury and soul wound is predominately controlled by the language of "injury" and "wound" rather than by the language of "soul" and the spiritual and theological dimensions most often associated with the soul's moral status. What about the language of sin? Of evil? Of bondage? Of estrangement? What views of forgiveness and reconciliation attach themselves to secular psychological and healthcare views? Does avoiding traditional language frames of morality and ethics make it more possible to deal with the intentions behind them? Or does it simply avoid the palpable urgencies of a tormented conscience begging to be understood in the actual spiritual consciousness of those suffering moral injury? In short, to be most effective in finding our way to healing our own and others' moral injury, it will be important to address the interplay between secular and religious discourse, as each is (or is not) efficacious in apprehending the lived truths being engaged.

There is one more aspect or limitation to medicalizing the term *moral injury*. Injured people are now special cases. They need to be treated for their injuries. Once they become patients, they are subjected to a whole array of protocols, roles, professionals, and extraordinary environments such as hospitals, clinics, and therapy rooms. In short, to medicalize a moral injury is to make moral injury atypical and special rather than a normal and ordinary part of daily living in a morally saturated and morally flawed world. This book will argue that we do a great disservice to one another—and especially to our military veterans—by segregating those with moral struggles from the rest of us in order to treat them as special cases. While on the one hand, providing special care for injured parties is laudable and sometimes necessary, on the other hand our discourse and metaphors may undermine the human solidarity necessary to address the common moral conundrums we all face. The more we can mainstream our moral discourse and share our moral failings and flaws in a realistic and nurturing public context, the greater the chance of amelioration and repair. And, more importantly, the relational, communal, and personal resources that will come into place will take us a long way beyond the isolation and hostilities generated by moral injury. In this writing, I hope to blend the strengths and account for the limits of multiple discourses about moral living. I will draw upon the metaphors "moral injury" and "moral healing" where they illuminate and guide. I will correct for them when they eclipse or avoid other important dimensions.

CHAPTER 3

I Am as We Are: From Hierarchies to Ensembles

I t is incorrect to think that our values are inside us. They are in fact between us. Whatever we come to think and feel about right and wrong is a result of countless complex interactional processes. Whatever we bring to any interaction is changed by that interaction. Moral distress and moral advance arise from the interaction between our internal worlds and the pressures or opportunities coming to us through our environments.

The Social Self: Resources from the West

Classical European and American views of the self, and American Protestantism in particular, have had a very difficult time accepting that the personal and the social are two sides of the same coin. We simply assume we are personally unique by nature and social by choice. And, worse, there continues to be a dominant notion that to be social is to diminish our personal well-being and to dilute or pollute our core essence. In the moral calculus of many European Americans, self-reliance and individualism are higher goods than collective engagement, unless collective engagement can be mobilized to serve our personal self-realization.

In contrast, this book recognizes that what goes on between humans, and between humans and our world, is made possible by social dynamics, properly understood and properly managed. Everything about us is social and interactional—always.

While individualism has dominated in the West, certain theologians and philosophers have offered alternative views of the human self as far more social. Karl Barth recognized that humans created in the image of God were thoroughly social; we were not personal and social, but unalterably relational. He identified the human situation as being under the conditions of "I am as thou art."[1] Each human being's welfare and each human's difficulties are irrevocably tied to each other. For Barth, to be co-human in the mode of "I am as thou art" was marked by "mutual looking one another in the eye," "mutual speaking and listening," and "mutual rendering of assistance." And, for Barth, to be human meant that such mutual looking, speaking, listening, and rendering assistance are enacted from a position of joy rather than resentment or obligation.

While Barth and others such as Martin Buber offer the beginnings of a social anthropology in which to ground our reflection about morality and moral injury, other twentieth- and twenty-first-century theologians have developed this social vision far more comprehensively. Liberation theologians, such as Gustavo Gutiérrez, asserted that sin and evil were not merely the result of individual wrongdoing but were deeply institutional, structural, and systemic. Process and feminist theologians and philosophers including John Cobb, Marjorie Suchocki, Catherine Keller, Rita Brock, and Sallie McFague have long argued for a view of the universe as interconnected and a vision of both God and humanity as thoroughly social realities. These perspectives have strongly rejected unbridled individualism and have argued that both human injury and human potential emerge from the social and interactive matrices of life. Unmitigated self-reliance has no future with them.[2]

I Am as We Are: African and Native American Challenges and Resources

Increasingly, the West has also been exposed to views from around the globe that go beyond individualistic self-realization in novel ways. While being deeply influenced by the Western challenges to individualism mentioned above, my thinking has been shaped as well by these non-Western perspectives. I draw upon these resources to illuminate what I mean in this book by the aphorism "I am as we are." This book is informed, in particular, by two non-Western sources that provide an expanded portrayal of the context of our human nature and moral capabilities. First, strands of African philosophy and religion maintain that "I am because we are and since we are, therefore I am."[3] Second, Native American perspectives emphasize that to be human is to be comprised at all times by "all our relations."[4]

I Am as We Are: From Hierarchies to Ensembles

Dr. Anne Kiome Gatobu is a Kenyan-American who was my advisee through three degree programs at Iliff School of Theology, including her doctoral degree. My conversations with Dr. Gatobu over the years opened my eyes to what it means to be immersed in a communal culture in which the social group takes precedence over the individual. Rather than diminishing individuality, I came to see that rich and full personhood is made possible by deeply belonging to a community and its ancestors. I learned from Dr. Gatobu that a village does more than raise its children; the village generates and maintains the very existence of the children and all its members. And the values, relationships, patterns of living, and sense of connection with the Creator and the community are all part of the same piece of cloth. There is no distinction between religion and culture. "Religion guides the morals, attitudes, relations, and actions of each individual with the community....What is important is the better-ment of the community and that the morals and virtues guide the relations between families and others."[5] At the same time, behavior is shaped by personal experiences and the community receives the benefit of individual personal experience. "Reli-gion...is not a static factor in a person's life....It calls for reshaping, renegotiating, repressing, rekindling and transforming integral symbolism and therefore it impacts our comprehension of life experiences."[6] Indeed, "I am because we are" is a dynamic constellation of interconnections enduring and expanding through life and commu-nity for the betterment of personal and social living.

One does not have to travel to Europe or Africa to discover that "I am as we are." The land on which the United States takes residence is peopled by indigenous groups who also live in unity with the Creator, Land, Sky, and Community. The aphorism by which this dynamic interplay is understood is "all our relations." For over thirty-five years, I have been a colleague and friend of Professor Tink Tinker, a Lutheran pastor and member of the Osage Nation. He has never failed to challenge Western individualism about cultural rights and communal vitalities based upon the Native worldview of participatory embeddedness in "*all* our relations." Later in the book I will illustrate how Tinker used "all our relations" as the touchstone of his consultation with the United Methodist Church to assist in healing the moral injury arising from its participation in the colonialization of Native Americans.[7] But first, I want to link the social character of human existence in Native American thought to the moral climate that this book assumes to bear upon us all.

To use the phrase "all our relations" is to comprehensively respect and balance all that exists in Creation and Community, including the forces of wind, rocks, ani-mals, people, and the seasons of nature. In Tinker's words, "...the phrase includes all the nations of the nations of the Two-Leggeds, the Four-Leggeds, the Wingeds, and all the Living-Moving Things of the Earth. A translation of *mitakuye oyasin* ["all our relations"] would better read, 'For all the above me and below me and around me things.'"[8] Egalitarian reciprocity, rather than authoritarian hierarchies, is the organizing center of Native American practice. The egalitarian character of "all our relations" is symbolized by a circle that people join and leave as welcomed participants. Rather than symbolizing our social life in historical terms, which prizes endings and progress, Native Americans symbolize life spatially where beginnings and endings and progress are of secondary importance. Rather, reciprocity, equal status, egalitarian access, and balance of elements in a spatially defined, dynamically open, and changing circle creates the moral context for living well with "all our relations," and not just with "our kind."

The centrality of reciprocity and balance are particularly critical with respect to engaging the inherent violence necessary for living in the world. From destroying one form of life in hunting or harvesting to gather food to taking life in war, violence is part of the circle of life. To maintain the circle and keep balance, reciprocal rituals of remorse and gratitude are required.[9] The moral climate is kept intact through these rituals and the balance of "all our relationships" is secured. Again, our values are not just individual internalizations, but public and communal engagements mediated through ritual and cultural practices within "all our relations."

The link of "all our relations" to violence is especially critical for our work on healing from moral injury. Moral injury most often involves some form of violence to self and/or others. Restoring the broken moral order is the main goal of healing, and it rests on an acknowledgement that one is both an actor and a recipient of violence and violation. Normalizing responsibility for our life in the world is in itself a moral challenge. The insights from Native American practices about restoring the balance of life through acknowledgment and reciprocity will prove valuable for practices outside the Native American context.

I do not select these examples of the social character of moral engagement to co-opt non-Western viewpoints, or to presume that the dominant American culture can or should become Native American or African. Respect for cultural differences and cultural integrity is required more than ever in today's conflicted national and global milieus. Cultural borrowing and cultural difference are moral issues in their own right. Neither do I present these views to analyze the strengths and weaknesses of cultural worldviews impinging on one another. Rather, I present these alternatives to demonstrate that over the eons human beings have inherited rich moral traditions and practices necessary for personal and communal well-being. Human nature is unalterably social and connective. Moreover, these alternative views both challenge dominant ideas and offer insights that can deepen the possibilities for new understandings more appropriate for the world's current situation. In addition, though the West has emphasized individual moral responsibility to the neglect of the communal and contextual, it is also laced with rich social and communal resources that can be brought to the foreground to enhance our moral endeavors. Attention to alternative visions may also help persons who reside within dominant Western traditions to recognize subordinated resources within their own historical contexts.

What follows in this book is a specification of the social character of human moral action underlying moral dissonance, dilemmas, injury, and healing. I will weave these various social-communal perspectives from the West, African, and Native American sources into a contemporary view of collaborative engagement of moral concerns. A collaborative relationship between Western and non-Western perspectives contributes to our goal of preventing moral injury and healing from its consequences.

To get the most from this book, it is necessary to discipline and revise how one thinks and acts. This book is not about information; it is about the everyday moral lives of individuals and communities. One habit of mind the reader will need to lose is the hierarchical mindset that we attach to our personal and social values. There is an intrinsic human drive to arrange virtues in a top-down value hierarchy (e.g., love is higher than friendship because it does not require reciprocity, and both love and friendship are higher than libido because they are not limited by bodily instincts). And we also create hierarchies of virtuous suffering. Suffering chosen to redeem others who are more vulnerable than ourselves is usually ranked highest, and the suffering of an oppressor ranks lowest.

I, thus, plot a different course than one that takes us up and down a presumed hierarchy of moral virtue and moral injury. To be sure, not all suffering inflicted and received is equal. Moral injury is very particular, and it accrues to individuals and social groups in differential ways. Marking difference does not require hierarchical arrangements, however. We can affirm intersections between various persons and groups who suffer, while also marking unique experiences calling for understanding and change.[10] Rather than thinking hierarchically, we have to think more laterally. Failure to think laterally can, in fact, perpetrate moral injury and harm. Hierarchical thinking risks separating us from the human bonds and creativity necessary for change and healing. A better model is the jazz ensemble or symphony orchestra. Each element of an orchestra or ensemble is a receptor and an agent; the quality of each participant, including the audience, accounts for the quality of the experience and the outcomes achieved. What happens between the composer, conductor, musicians, and audience is a contextually creative collaborative process.[11]

In Tapiwa Mucherera's work, the concept of "Palaver" offers a helpful entry to a concrete, non-hierarchical way of being with one another in the face of moral challenges (as well as other difficulties). And while the collaborative conversation approach I utilize derives from the West, it gains illumination from Mucherera's Shona context. When he was a PhD candidate at Iliff and the University of Denver, Mucherera urged the community to engage through Palaver as a means of ameliorating serious conflict tearing us apart. I was impressed with what he taught us, and

Palaver's power in our community life. Since that time, I have tried to incorporate some the features of Palaver into my own work and mindset.

Mucherera taught us that a Palaver is "an informal gathering usually for the purposes of providing counsel and support for those facing personal, family and/or community crisis and problems, and sometimes for the purposes of education and to share joys."[12] Palaver is a way of being in the world, beyond problem-solving and healing, though it serves the ends of responding to moral challenges and healing moral injury. In Palaver everyone has a place and a voice. Mutual speaking and listening are protected and enhanced. Problem-solving emerges from the interaction rather than formulated from outside or above and imposed on the participants. All members can contribute to the conversation as a resource, not as a critic or judge.[13] The key features of Palaver, which are reflected in the approach this book takes, include honestly naming the problem, reevaluating the interpretative schemata maintaining the problem, exploring the negative consequences of the problem, and reformulating new understandings and practices for addressing the problem.[14] All of this takes place in a social process in which various levels of status and authority find voice, but none alone determines the outcome.

To summarize and conclude, moral values do not reside within individuals alone. They arise from interactions between various communities and individual psyches. Understanding moral challenges, including moral injury and moral healing, requires Westerners to change their habits of mind and social practices. African and Native American resources provide a stimulus and encouragement to take this step. In the sections below, I will develop and "operationalize" what it means to think in terms of "I am as we are" with respect to engaging moral dissonance, moral dilemmas, moral injuries, and moral healing. Selected features of Palaver will illuminate elements of "contextual creativity," the core to moral healing.

For Further Reading

Benkler, Yochai. *The Penguin and the Leviathan: The Triumph of Cooperation over Self-Interest*. New York: Crown Business, 2011.

Coleman, Monica A. *Creating Women's Theology: A Movement Engaging Process Thought*. Eugene, OR: Pickwick, 2011.

Keller, Catherine. *Face of the Deep: A Theology of Becoming*. London: Routledge, 2007.

CHAPTER 4

Anchor Points

Building on the social views of the human self and an interconnected world, three anchor points emerge to ground my approach to moral guidance and healing. These are the core elements that I continually return to as we move from injury to healing. The first anchor point is "Contextual Creativity." The second is "Habits of Mind." The third is "Strategic Examples." Together, all the main features of this book conceptually and practically come into focus.

Anchor Point 1— Contextual Creativity

Contextual creativity is the unending capacity of groups and individuals to influence their lives and environments in novel ways. The universe itself is contextually creative. Theologically, the idea of contextual creativity is another word for human freedom, agency, autonomy, and self-realization. It is the basis for dignity and resistance in the face of evil ("my head is bloody, but unbowed")[1] as well as for imagining and creating new configurations of personal and social life ("I have a dream!").[2] Contextual creativity is the built-into-life basis for human morality. Our moral advances as individuals and groups are made possible by our innate capacity for contextual creativity. Contextual creativity is also the capacity to make choices that lead to moral injury; it does not always result in good or life-giving outcomes. And, most importantly for this writing, contextual creativity is the vital element in healing past moral injuries and fashioning new moral compasses to guide the future. In short, because of contextual creativity we must affirm two dissonant truths: "Humans will always screw things up" and "Where there is life, there is hope."[3]

Contextual creativity is both a concept and an activity. As a concept, it offers the realistic certainty that the universe supports progress even in the face of demise. As an activity, it says something about the relentless capacity to direct our agency, to some extent, in everything we do. Here we place a larger emphasis upon contextual creativity as an activity than as a concept. When tempted to despair in the face of intractable "stuckness" and overwhelming pain, reminding oneself that contextual creativity is an inextinguishable element of life can sustain endurance and empower resistance.[4]

In this book, contextual creativity is a resource for addressing moral dissonance, moral dilemmas, and moral injury. The collaborative process of moral healing is built upon the concept and practice of contextual creativity. There are four interacting activities that tie contextual creativity to addressing moral dissonance, dilemmas, injury, and healing. These four activities are naming, framing, enacting, and revising our moral histories. I will provide a brief description of these factors now to anchor the reader succinctly in a complex set of ideas and practices that will appear often in fuller detail throughout the book.

Naming our moral dissonance, dilemmas, and injuries is an act of courage. Identifying the truth of our inner lives and moral actions to ourselves and to others is often shaming and terrifying. Creating safe climates for naming our moral truths and exploring them in an empowering rather than condemning manner is at the heart of naming one's truth. Before we can change our moral narratives, we must name them as honestly and "feelingly" as we can.

Framing what we name is the basis for changing the power of the past. Naming alone is not enough. It can lead to "analysis paralysis," and even to a sense of futile self-judgment and helplessness. When we frame what we name in actionable and benevolent terms, we begin to gain the power to resist, change, and heal our moral narratives and our moral histories. Contextual creativity is action-oriented. Hence, when we frame our moral realities in actionable terms, based on a sense of benevolence toward self and others, change is already taking place.

But naming and framing alone are insufficient. We also must enact something new: to engage ourselves and others in terms of the goals we envision in the reframing of our moral situation. This is where moral problem-solving and social engagement arise. It is a process of trial and error. Social support, communal solidarity, strategic public advocacy, and exploring alternative internal meanings and codes are part of the enacting dimension of contextual creativity.

Finally, there are always outcomes from what we do and how we do it. The outcomes must be received—named—and incorporated into individual and community self-understanding. This is when contextual creativity leads to a revision of one's moral orientation and behaviors, and sometimes to one's total self-understanding and social identification. Changing moral narratives means creating new moral histories: naming the world differently and responding to it from our new or reset moral compasses. This is the phase where moral changes have to be anchored in self and community so that they are available as resources for what happens next.

Anchor Point 2—Habits of Mind: How to Read This Book

To engage in naming, framing, enacting, and revising requires discipline and the development of habits of mind and spirit.[5] In this book, I aim to help the reader develop specific ways of thinking in relation to addressing moral dissonance, dilemmas, and injuries. To get the most out of this book I am asking the reader *not* to do five things. I am then asking the reader to *commit* to doing five specific things.

The first "not to" is to expect an answer or position on a given moral challenge facing us in today's church and world. You will not find an argued position about any contemporary moral position in this book. I am not here to convince you to take a particular moral stance about the critical issues of our day.

The second "not to" is to think that you will find more harmonious relationships as a result of reading this book. You might or might not. It is a guide to understanding intractable moral dissonance and to living better within it. It will not necessarily lead to greater moral harmony and compatibility. Sometimes moral action destabilizes harmonious situations. It might not reconcile you to yourself. Sometimes moral healing is not possible; living well with chronic moral pain may be the best outcome possible for you at this time.

The third "not to" is to expect that you can read this book without doing a great amount of personal work. There is no free ride here. Moral health and moral healing take effort.

The fourth "not to" is to assume that you will discover an underlying unity within the conflicting points of view in the moral challenges that you are facing. We live in a world where there are divergent moral choices and moral styles. There are irreconcilable moral differences. Difference is not always a matter of misunderstanding. Some differences are principled and noble. Some are destructive and toxic. They may be in a life-and-death opposition to one another. How these differences are recognized and lived out is a major critical challenge of our day and we need a lot more engagement and trial and error to recognize this and live as well as we can within our moral cauldrons.

The fifth "not to" is to assume that moral dissonance, failure, and injury are stronger realities than moral goodness and healing. Certainly moral responsibility and theological and spiritual integrity require that we accurately name the truth about moral dissonance, moral failure, and moral injury. But at the same time it is much more important that we embrace the greater faith we have in the power of moral engagement to heal and improve life. The human drive to survive requires moral clarity and healing. The Christian faith affirms, "Love is stronger than death." The Christian faith witnesses to the actual on-the-ground reality that trespasses are forgivable and transformable into greater moral good. This is a book about hope, not moral despair.

What five things must you "commit" to in reading this book? First, you must re-read difficult passages, take notes, read the footnotes, and check out the supplemental resources identified along the way. You should take a considerable amount of time to immerse yourself in the book. I regard this book as a conversation partner with which to engage and reengage collaboratively.

Second, you must put these ideas to work in the concrete details and challenges of your life. Try them out in practice. Journal about them. Moral living and moral healing are about behaviors, concepts, and ritual practices on the ground. They are not primarily about an author's point of view in a book. You will do best by making them your own. Put these materials to work in practices in your daily living and see what happens. Adapt them to your style and circumstances. These practices include prayer, worship, consultation, education, self-awareness, self-compassion, and self-regulation, as well as your direct behaviors with those you are enacting in your world. It involves deep and open conversations with others. Joining your past wisdom, successes, and failures with the views of this book will not provide "answers" but it will, without doubt, provide richness and generate new directions for you—but only if you do your part with as much effort as it took me to get this book into your hands.

Third, for this book to work for you, you must give yourself permission not to change unless you really want to. I honestly did not write this book to change anyone. In my view, change is something to receive as a result of attentive living rather than something to orchestrate based on analysis and conviction.

Fourth, for this book to work for you as I intend, you must commit yourself to genuinely engage the moral perspectives of those whose values offend you the most. If it is a fact of spiritual life and human nature that our destinies are intertwined, our moral discourse must always be with people whose dignity we respect in all circumstances, even when we are unalterably opposed to some of their values and behaviors toward us. Our enemies are humans, as devilish as they may sometimes behave. Loving enemies, in the very least, means engaging our enemies with the same respect we believe that they owe us. Because they do not offer that respect to us does not foreclose on our extending it to them. Love only becomes stronger than death when we act lovingly.

Fifth, for this book to work for you, a radical trust in the power of life will be required. What I have in mind is more than an idea about radical trust. What I am calling for is an *attitude* of radical trust in all we do. For the world to endure, and for humans to survive and flourish, it is incumbent upon us to spiritually join with the powers of life that have brought the universe into being and eventuated in human life, love, and goodness. An attitude, conviction, and habit of mind characterized by radical trust will enable us to join up with these efficacious energies. The powers of life mediated through nature, culture, religious faith and practice, and intense human struggle, will guide and reform our moral living, prevent moral injury, and empower healing from moral wounding.

Anchor Point 3— Strategic Examples of Commitment to the Concrete

While theology and theories of the self are important and habits of mind are necessary, a central assertion of pastoral theology and care is that these must always be grounded in the concrete, the realities of everyday experience. I provide numerous strategic examples throughout the book in order to help the reader weave their own moral tapestry in the dissonances and dilemmas they face—and to reweave the tapestry frayed or damaged by moral injury. I have selected strategic moral examples of how people similar to those reading this book are engaging the moral challenges in their situations. I do not present these strategic examples as templates of what the reader "ought to do" in their own lives, or how caregivers ought to structure their caregiving. I offer these as examples to illustrate some of the theoretical and practical wisdom distilled in the book. I also offer them as examples of skills some people use to develop more vital moral living. Most importantly, I offer them as mirrors and talking points for the reader to enter the collaborative space this book tries to introduce as a productive model of contextually creative moral responsiveness. From the conversation generated between the reader and these strategic examples I expect that the reader will feel less alone and will discover avenues of thought and action not previously considered. If this happens, the strategic examples will become a resource for contextually and creatively naming, framing, enacting, and revising the reader and caregiver's moral situations.

There is more than an educational benefit to strategic examples. There is also a healing benefit. One of the dimensions of moral struggles is their shaming and isolating effects. When our vulnerabilities are exposed, we feel "naked and ashamed." The natural response to these feelings is to hide. We cut ourselves off from the feelings and memories, or we try to minimize them. We assume that we can and must handle them ourselves. Exposing them to others feels like another level of shame. Our mantra, whether clearly stated or not, is "I can bear it if I don't share it."

This book takes the opposite view. Central to healing moral wounds is to find the proper context and means of sharing them. Healing moral injuries requires us to punctuate the shame and isolation by exposing ourselves to trustworthy others in a context of repair and correction. The mantra of this book is, "If we can share it, we can bear it." Sharing, in the form of naming our moral situation, is the first (and biggest) step toward breaking out of the prison of moral demise.

The strategic examples that I share often break taboos against telling the truth to ourselves—and about ourselves.[6] Those stories (including my own) that appear in the strategic examples disclose the power of breaking out of shame and isolation and of finding ways to courageously engage sometimes excruciatingly painful matters with strength, grace, and hope. Sharing and retelling one's story is not endless paddling in the victim's end of the pool. Sharing is a strength-based platform for enacting new alternatives for living: taking realistic account of our particular moral past and, with the help of others, constructing a meaningful future, morally speaking. The strategic examples that I provide illuminate anchor points to serve as stimuli for healing moral injury and revising moral compasses.

Some readers will do best with this book if they read through all the strategic examples before tackling the other sections. Not only will such a reading engage "real people" and "practical situations," it may prepare the mind to better track with the conceptual elements and suggestions for caregiving articulated throughout the book. It might also help the reader get started earlier on the work for which they are seeking this book's assistance.

Strategic Example: Reverend Lawson's Abuse Reporting Dilemma

Pastoral work is thoroughly infused with moral dissonance and dilemmas, both for ministers and those they serve. Pastors face unending expectations to act spontaneously in complex and ambiguous moral climates. There is no escaping moral stress in the practice of ministry! Knowing the situation and trusting one's relational bonds enables pastors to be more (rather than less) effective.

A pastoral colleague presented to a consultation group a complex pastoral situation fraught with several layers of moral dissonance. The case that follows is an imaginative elaboration of a pastoral situation related to clergy confidentiality and mandatory reporting. It is used with permission.[7]

Rev. Jennifer Lawson is the minister of a growing, mostly white suburban church on the liberal spectrum of American Protestantism. She is beloved in her community. Her church is characterized by strong preaching that combines attention to personal spiritual growth, education, and social justice-oriented service. Before her second career as a minister, she was a recognized authority on the prevention of sexual and domestic violence. Rev. Lawson is an emotionally open person. She is aware of the boundaries required of ministers in relationship with those they serve. She is also a self-discloser who uses her own experience publicly to strengthen her bonds with her congregation and show how "we are all in this faith thing together." The church is thriving and growing on all fronts. People trust her with their lives, including disclosing sensitive personal matters.

Rev. Lawson asked her ministry support group to debrief an unsettling pastoral situation. At a recent church picnic, she overheard Mr. Thompson, a father of a member of her youth group, say to someone, "Well, he won't do that again!" She wasn't sure what this meant, but she was particularly drawn to the firmness, even anger, in the father's tone of voice. "What worried me about this," she said, "is that I had seen the son earlier at the picnic and noticed that he had a black eye and some bruises on his face. He seemed kind of down and withdrawn, which was unusual for him. Justin is normally the life of the party." She went on to say that she knew that there had been some tensions between the father and the son, and that physical violence could be a part of that. "Mrs. Thompson is in the prayer and support group that I lead, and she has asked us to pray for the family and especially for the tension between Mr. Thompson and Jason. She didn't say that there had been violence, but it was clear to us that she was afraid things could lead to that. Both were stubborn and were showing a lot of frustration with one another."

Rev. Lawson said she wasn't sure how to proceed at the picnic. She knew that reporting laws in her state required her to call the police if she witnessed or had reason to suspect that a child under sixteen was being physically neglected or abused. She was hesitant to call the police until she knew more about the source of the injury on Justin's face. She didn't want to alienate Mr. Thompson. She was also concerned that if she called the police, it would destabilize the family. There was the added worry that if she called the police and told them that Mrs. Thompson had feared physical violence that she would violate a confidence and jeopardize her pastoral relationship with Mrs. Thompson, and perhaps the whole family. "I felt like I was in a huge bind. On the one hand, I am legally required to report the suspicion of abuse and violence. On the other hand, I wasn't sure if there was enough evidence for me to do so. I was very anxious about the negative consequences of reporting. I could lose my relationship with Mrs. Thompson and the family, and make things even tenser in the family. Could I risk this?"

This dilemma was very difficult for Rev. Lawson. There was moral dissonance between her duty to report, maintaining a positive relationship with Mrs. Thompson, and not destabilizing the family. How should she adjudicate these conflicting moral claims? She decided that her duty to report had priority over her desire to maintain her relationship as it stood with Mrs. Thompson and the family. She believed that the best way to minister to the family, even though they might not accept her as their pastor if she reported the suspected abuse, was to address the abuse. She concluded in her mind that the family's long-term health depended on their stopping further violence if it was taking place, and to set up a healing milieu for the Thompson family.

Having settled the dissonance in herself, she approached Justin casually at the picnic. After chatting a bit, she asked him, "Justin, what happened to your face? It looks like you ran into a Mack truck." She said, "Justin kind of laughed, and said, 'It wasn't a truck. It was second base. I was trying to steal second base in our varsity game, and it didn't work out too well. I am okay, but it was pretty embarrassing. My dad had been angry at me for sliding headfirst into bases. He was afraid I would hurt myself. We argued about it. But I guess he was right after all."

Rev. Thompson was relieved to hear that the cause of the injury was from a baseball game. But she also wanted to learn a bit more to be sure. She later approached Mr. Thompson and asked how Justin got hurt. Mr. Thompson said, "He slid face-first into second base! I have been telling him not to slide headfirst, but he wouldn't listen. Now he knows better. I don't think that he will do that again!" Rev. Lawson said, "I am glad to see that he is alright. That could have been a lot worse."

In their conversations with Rev. Lawson on this ministry episode, her consultant group affirmed her anxiety and shared some of the murky boundary issues they experience and difficult judgments they are called to make. There was a lot of support for how difficult ministry can be when decisions to do the right thing at one level might cause harm and disruption at another level. Everyone was impressed with the way Rev. Lawson named the conflicts in the situation, including those within her own moral values, and came to a clear strategy for ministry in this situation. One of Rev. Lawson's takeaway insights is a teaching point to clergy: "The teaching moment is this: don't go off half-cocked. Drama can be intoxicating. The press of reporting alleged abuse can obscure the reasonable, oft-times benign, underlying story. This underscores the need for pastors to have a listening and discerning ear in a trusted colleague so that the moral dissonance can be fully parsed before action is taken." Another point to underscore is that the way the challenges of moral dissonance and moral dilemmas are handled can prevent moral injury or soul wounds. Great harm could have resulted for the Thompsons, for Rev. Lawson, and the congregation as a whole had she not competently managed this moral dilemma.

Habits of Mind Exercise: Collaborative Conversation

I am asking readers to develop new habits of mind as they encounter this book. There will be explicit sections dedicated to tracking one's inner thought processes with opportunity to modify and apply them strategically in the reader's own world.

The main habit of mind this book seeks to promote is skilled collaborative conversational engagement in life and ministry. "Collaborative conversation" will be described and illustrated over the course of the book. It is important to "anchor" the idea now. First, however, know that collaborative conversation is not the same as "cooperation," such as getting together to make a difficult task easier by sharing it. Rather, "collaborative conversation" is a mindset that determines how we engage information and data that comes to us. Collaborative engagement is being alive to the moment and connecting with whatever seems most vital and promising to you in that moment. What happens next takes care of itself, if the collaborative mindset is maintained. Thus, collaborative conversation is a matter of both grasping and creating efficacious knowledge that bears strategically on the moral dissonance, dilemmas, and injuries we face in the here and now.

Collaborative conversation centers on three habits of mind. First, collaborative conversation requires a disciplined habit of attuning to what is curious, exciting, interesting, and challenging to me as I receive new information and knowledge, however that knowledge may come to me. Second, collaborative conversation requires the disciplined habit of sharing openly without judgment and problem-solving agendas what was salient (interesting, curious, exciting, and challenging) to me in what I just experienced. Third, collaborative conversation requires ongoing attunement to the new meanings, thoughts, ideas, skills, and feelings that take their rise in the "in-between" space that is created by sharing knowledge and one's enlivened inner dialogue about it. This third element is where new knowledge and new resources for change come about. It is where the contextually creative elements of naming, framing, enacting, and revising find their energy and direction. Chapter 9 provides detailed guidance for employing collaborative processes in naming, framing, enacting, and revising moral issues.[8]

I recently came across a fascinating example of the way collaborative conversation in musical medicine resolved a medical crisis. Andrew Schulman writes of his experience in the surgical intensive care unit at Mount Sinai Beth Israel Hospital in New York.[9] Music had been the medium that had brought him back from a near-death experience. He wanted to pay back his gift by playing his guitar for patients in the ICU two or three times a week. He recounts an episode with an elderly black

– 33 –

musician, a well-known side-man in various jazz settings around New York City. Schulman stood by Mr. G.'s bed and began to play jazz music that Mr. G. would know. "Within a few minutes, the writhing slowed, and then stopped, and the pained expression on his face started to disappear. I had his attention." So far, one might think that Schulman did little more than enter a cooperative rather than collaborative process. But then his intuitive genius came into play. "He was listening to music he'd certainly played many times before. Now I wanted him to do more than listen. I wanted him to think about playing."

Without naming it as such, Schulman takes a collaborative turn at this point. "I switched from a solo style, left out the melody part, and began to play only the chords of the tunes. I wanted him to imagine an ensemble. . . . So I figured if I left out the melody and went to chords maybe that would send a signal to Mr. G. I moved to tunes with faster tempo." From this point, something quite remarkable took place. Mr. G.'s facial expression changed dramatically. "His eyes remained closed, but his brow began to furrow, just as a musician's would when he is deeply in the flow of playing. . . . It sure looked to me like Mr. G. was on a bandstand, playing his horn full tilt. The signal had gotten through. I'm convinced he was playing the melody."

Rather than supply the energy and resources for healing through a diagnosis-treatment model of care, Schulman evoked collaborative participation by creating the conditions where new energy emerged between the two players. This produced a new world and had a salutary healing effect on Mr. G. The nurse reported that he was without doubt moving past a medical crisis. "The music had done more than the sedatives had been able to accomplish. By getting Mr. G. to interact, he had reengaged in his life and reconnected to a core part of himself. He was pulling himself up from the bottom of the well."[10]

Schulman attributes this to the capacity of music to find its way to levels of the brain inaccessible through other means. "I saw how music reached beyond everything that was going on with him, mentally and physically, found his essence, and pulled him back." From the collaborative conversation standpoint of this book, the outcome was equally well-explained by what happened in the space between Schulman and Mr. G. Each brought something to the "bedside bandstand" and found ways creatively to respond to what excited and interested them. As a consequence, something novel came into place that grasped and transformed each of them in different ways. Schulman himself realized that this had less to do with imposing something on Mr. G. and more to do with the amazing contextual creativity that grew up between them together through the music they had shared in producing. "Somehow this had happened to me, too [when I was deathly sick like Mr. G.]. Music intervened for both of us, stabilized us, and enabled the doctors to do their job. It was impressive. And inspiring."[11]

Collaborative conversation creates spaces and enters those spaces with eyes for the new, the exciting, and the promising. Those spaces become, as for Schulman and

Mr. G., places of new power and possibility. It is important to note that there are two interlocking collaborative conversations going on in this event. First, there is the collaborative contextual creativity between Schulman and Mr. G. in their improvisational performance. Second, there is the collaboration between the music and the musician-patients as the music evokes new ranges of knowledge and experience in the service of healing the psyche and bonding persons to one another. Though this book uses moral engagement rather than music as the medium for collaborative participation in moral challenges, the interactive process is transferable.

It is precisely at this point where the discipline comes in, where new habits of mind are required. Most of our inner dialogue is not about what excites us. It is about what disappoints us. It is about what we wish were there, not about what we are alive to in ourselves or what interests us about what is in front of us. Or, it is about what we should do, or advise others to do, in the light of what we hear from them. Our minds become over inhabited by "yes... but." So, the first thing I am going to ask the reader to do in this initial habit of mind exercise is to tune out the part of your inner dialogue that focuses on what frustrated, disappointed, distracted, or blocked your curiosity and excitement in what you have read up until now. Lose the "yes... but!"

Next, I want you to think back over what you have read and answer these questions. What excited me about what I read in this book so far? Why did that excite me? Where were my values and perspectives challenged? What questions does it suggest for me to think about and explore? If I were to raise this with the author, what do I imagine he would say back? With whom do I need to talk to about this? Where is my body engaging this material? What is it saying to me that I best listen to and talk about?

Finally, what has emerged for you in this habits of mind exercise that seems promising to you? What is new? How is the "old" reaffirmed? Where does it lead you? What steps will you take to get yourself there? Make a specific commitment to an action that you can take and from which you will commit yourself to learn what you did not know before.

For Further Reading

Lewis, Michael. *The Undoing Project: A Friendship That Changes Our Minds*. New York: Norton, 2017.

Schwartz, John. "Katharine Hayhoe, a Climate Explainer Who Stays Above the Storm." *New York Times* October 11, 2016. www.nytimes.com/2016/10/11 /science/katharine-hayhoe-climate-change-science.html

Part II
Moral Challenges

Introduction to Part II

Wobbly Gyroscopes

Moral orientations guiding our actions in specific times and places have come into place through centuries of distilled thought and practices in response to events situated in history, nature, and culture. Together, these enculturated moral orientations comprise our internalized and habitual macrosystemic moral gyroscopes. They make survival and progress possible over time. When we are harmed by the actions of other individuals and groups, as well as by the catastrophes of the natural environment, the press to survive, heal, and retaliate is in accordance with the moral mechanisms necessary to hold others accountable and to preserve our existence as individuals and groups. These capacities constitute the moral environment within which individuals, communities, and political entities must set their moral compasses, regulate their relationships with one another, and correct their courses.

But macrosystemic moral orientations are not only enduring; they are conflicted and unstable. They wobble and contend. As we will see below, the theological and moral assessment of the concept of God in monotheistic cultures presents a variety of conflicting interpretations, requiring assessment and choice. The doctrine of God in relation to concrete events is wobbly; in some cases it is a sustaining and healing reality while in other cases it is unusable or even harmful. So, too, our immersion in nature, history, and culture gives rise to conflicting theories about how to live in the cosmos and to organize our individual and group lives in the most morally positive way. Much of the moral dissonance, dilemmas, and injury we face today takes its rise because of irreconcilable differences within the macrosystemic moral orientations into which we are enculturated.

Take one common example: Gender. Our bodies are given very specific values by cultural norms about what it means to be male and female. Gender identity is not just a personal enterprise. Nor is it purely biological. Rules for bodily actions such as pleasure, procreation, aggression, and mobility are mostly determined by our historical and cultural contexts. Fulfilling these expectations is a moral good; violating them is morally unacceptable. Our moral compasses are preset, though adjusted or modified over time as historical and cultural circumstances change. Dissonance and dilemmas arise from contending macrosystemic values of what it means to be male and female. Moral injury and moral healing take place in relation to how we interpret, fulfill, and revise these cultural conventions.

To take another example, a veteran healing from moral injuries incurred in war requires sustained attention to factors of history and culture. War is not just a personal enterprise. It is a monumental historical cataclysm, mediated through contending cultural and political values. Individuals are cultivated and recruited by their groups to be warfighters. They enter war because they believe it is a good or moral thing to do, given the alternatives facing them. Moral dissonance arises for veterans when they begin to question the actions that they took (or failed to take) on behalf of their community in specific times and places. Moral injury results when they conclude that they did the wrong thing, or did the right thing in the wrong way. Thus, the intensely challenging moral injuries borne by individual military personnel are also historical and cultural productions, fraught with countless personal and social difficulties. Without decision and actions made in time and community, moral injury is not possible. So, also, without resources and perspectives conveyed by cultures in specific times and places moral healing is not possible. History and culture are therefore part and parcel of our moral conundrums arising from war and all else. In short, there is no way to disconnect the personal and the public in understanding moral injury and fashioning healing responses to it.[1]

The notion of macrosystemic moral gyroscopes, as massive and enduring as they are, should not be regarded in mechanistic terms. Our moral guidance systems are interactive energy centers. They receive, distill, revise, and replace specific moral codes and moral practices over time in the light of compelling local circumstances. I think of our moral capacities as moral organisms, operating much like oysters who receive and are nourished by the waters of the sea. In turn, they cleanse and restore the quality of the waters through which they receive and give life. Without our human capacities for contextual creativity and adaptability, moral living and moral healing would not be possible; atrophy, trivia, chaos, and brokenness would be our lot.

The actual values we hold and the practices we enact are highly contextual and dynamic. They have meaning in local circumstances but frequently contend with other local practices and the larger common good. The gyroscopes that mark our moral standpoints and the compasses that guide our courses are inherently unsteady. They offer more than one direction, and become destabilized by contending alternatives. The gyroscopes we use are wobbly instruments. Identifying the proper tools, setting and resetting our courses, and correcting misguided directions are inescapable dimensions of learning to do the right thing and to heal from doing the wrong thing (and from having the wrong thing done to us).

In part II, I want to examine how the very compasses we use are in themselves moral challenges as well as moral resources. To live well morally it behooves us to name our foundational resources, frame their gifts as well as their problems in actionable terms, enact their possibilities in concrete living, and reset our moral bearings as guides for ourselves and others. Attending to the various moral challenges we face will provide a basis for vital living and healing the soul's wounds.

God as Moral Conundrum

There is no way for Christians to address our struggles with moral dissonance, moral dilemmas, moral injury, and moral healing without engaging the idea of God. The inherited teachings about God in monotheistic cultures such as Christianity, Judaism, and Islam assert that God is the very basis of the moral capacities necessary to guide our life in the world. To put it blatantly, whether one believes in God or not, or whether one identifies with a religious tradition or not, the mental and moral furniture of all parties in monotheistic cultures has a "God label" on it somewhere. There is not only one idea of God, agreed upon by all. Indeed, just as we explored alternative conceptions of the human self earlier, this text will articulate emergent alternatives to what has been the dominant notion of God in Christianity. But, whatever their form, these varied ideas of God contribute to the moral machinery of our lives, positively or negatively. Even in our secular age, they continue to have impact on our moral sensibilities and our moral struggles.

This chapter will explore how our understandings of God impact our moral sense of self and how they contribute, sometimes, to our moral dissonance as well as to the possibility of moral healing. I will first focus on what has been broadly taken to be the traditional or classical Christian idea of God. This has certainly been contested and there are alternatives to this traditional notion. However, many persons with whom we engage, as caregivers and sympathetic conversation partners, continue to live out of these conceptions and their implications for our moral understandings. It is, thus important, to explore these notions in some depth. I will both try to positively elaborate this classical view in relation to our moral concerns as well as raise issues about where it can contribute to moral dissonance and injury.

God as Moral Architect

In traditional Christian teaching, God the creator is the architect of the moral machinery necessary to become the kind of human beings God intends for us to become and to live well with one another and the earth. In terms of our earlier discussion, we are created by God to be in life-enhancing engagements with "all our relations." God brought forth human beings to live responsibly with one another, to respect the limits of knowledge of good and evil, and to care for the world that cares for us.

Central moral affirmations of Christianity have included that God is righteous, loving, and just. For Christians, God's righteousness, love, and justice are found most decisively in the New Testament and early Church witness to Jesus of Nazareth. Through Jesus, God's love is disclosed as embodied self-giving for the restoration of a world caught up in moral injury, even moral death. Divine love, embodied in the life of the world as witnessed to in Jesus Christ, creates enduring communities of justice, love, and blessing. It heals the broken, liberates the oppressed, and lays the framework for righteous communities. But God's creative and redemptive love is not limited to individuals and communities. It restores the cosmos and influences its unfolding and fulfillment. God's loving presence in the life of the world is the basis for all contextually creative loving and just relationships; it is the base from which we bring about vital personal, communal, and ecophilial living. When we seek to be moral creatures in our everyday living, we are attuning to the moral machinery given to us by virtue of our creation as humans in the image of God.

Building on these classical insights, relational justice can be allied with love as the central moral value intended by God. Love is not one thing, justice another. Relational justice is the norm by which love in the image of God is measured or realized. "Relational justice points to shalom, or rightness of relationship and well-being between creator, creatures, and the people of God. Just relationality opposes injustice that takes the form of coercion, denigration, marginalization, and devaluation of created life, including human life."[1] Relational justice seeks to find terms in which "all our relations" may thrive and be in mutually beneficial and co-equal relationships rather than exploitive dominant-subordinate ones:

> Against the destructiveness of domination, relational justice promotes the values of egalitarian mutuality and ecological sustainability. Relational justice leads to shalom and celebration of the harmonious relationships established between God and humans, among humans, and between all entities of the ecosystem.[2]

When we participate in realizing relational justice in all our relationships, we reflect the image of a righteous, loving, and just God.

If one's moral architecture derives from these traditional teachings about God, four additional factors that have been part of this idea must be taken into account. First, the idea of divine mystery, or holiness, frees us from presumptions and moral superiority toward others. Second, the ideas of God as enduring and ever-present assure us of the lasting consequences of our moral contributions. Third, linking concepts of righteousness and holiness to God and moral living requires us to "mind the righteousness gap" that can become a source of moral dissonance and injury rather than a source of love and relational justice. Fourth, we must not let the otherness of God as enduring holy mystery in relation to the world eclipse the irreducible embodiment of all life and the unity of soul, body, and community in our moral endeavors.

First, God's holiness and mystery are foundational to all moral engagements and moral healing. To say that God is disclosed in the New Testament witness to Jesus of Nazareth is not to presume that humans, including Christian humans, have final authoritative knowledge about the being or specific will of God. God is mystery who stands always in freedom and novelty in relation to everything else. To recognize God's otherness—God's holiness—is to embody a humble expectation for surprise and discovery and challenge. We cannot reduce God, others, or ourselves to our own categories of value and meaning. This insight was precisely what drove the neo-orthodox theologian Karl Barth to stand against Hitler and what Barth saw as the idolatry of Nazism. The mystery of God requires us always to see the mystery and "out-of-reach" dimensions within others and ourselves. It is in this "in-between" space of knowledge and mystery that new energies for moral living, including healing from moral injury, come into place.

Second, because God is creative and enduring, as well as present and empowering, we can expect our moral efforts to have lasting effect. They are not ephemeral shots in the dark that may or may not have consequence beyond our actions. They arise from the empowering energies of God and the universe, and they are preserved as building blocks for future possibilities. Nothing is lost in the life of God. Nor is it ever too late in the kingdom of God. What we do or fail to do makes a difference and endures, whether we perceive it or not. Positively stated, trusting the powers of life, of God, frees us to explore new options for relational justice, creative loving, and ecological vitality.

Third, we have to take care to "mind the righteousness gap" in our moral endeavors. "Minding the gap" is taken from rail transportation culture.[3] When trains pull into a station to exchange passengers, there is a gap between the station platform and the train. Very bad things happen if people fall into the gap. "Minding the gap" is a call to be very careful in a dangerous situation. In moral living, there is a large potential for the concept of "righteousness" to create a dangerous gap between God and humans, and between one another. If "righteousness" is seen as moral superiority and attainable by only a few, then it sets up an "in" and an "out" group and many other forms of moral dissonance. It can be a source of considerable moral injury when one group brings condemnation upon another because they do not meet the standards of righteousness of the judging group. Or views of God's judgmental righteousness may lead to despair about oneself or rejection of others. The "righteousness gap" is a deadly gap. It bears careful minding.

I believe that much of the move away from Christianity in the contemporary United States is related to this "righteousness gap." Many feel that God is not loving or just, but punishing and critical. And many have moved away from the church because, whether in its conservative or liberal forms, it has erected a variety of "scales of righteousness" by which to evaluate one another judgmentally. It is morally injurious to construct our relationships to God and to one another based on scales of righteousness that work against love, relational justice, and human solidarity. This book is an attempt to bring a theology of God's righteousness in terms of compassionate love and relational justice to bear on everything we do in "all our relations." As such, it will challenge, and hopefully contribute to healing from, the righteousness gap that hurts us so much and prevents the kind of healing and positive moral living toward which we are drawn.

Fourth, I have been articulating a tradition-based theology of God as the creative source of a morally good physical universe. But even at this stage, it is important to add caveats. We must take special care to recognize that human bodies and human bodily activities are positive sites and instruments of moral living. The body is the basis for our capacity to be fully human in the image of God. Classical Christian ideas of God as spirit and mystery and as "wholly other" have led directly to moral injury. Failure to affirm and enhance the embodied nature of life in the universe and the unity of soul, body, and community is at the core of a great deal of moral self-denigration of and by persons, communities, cultures, and history. If there is a "righteousness gap" in Christianity, there is a Grand Canyon-size chasm between body, soul, and environment in our cherished theological traditions and ecclesial practices. This book will depart from much of classical Christian theology to offer a firm alternative to the pervasive split of spirit, body, soul, history, and community that cause and result in moral injury. Instead, this book links divine love and relational justice to embodied life in the material world created and being brought forth by an incarnate, material, embodied God.[4] In a word, to heal wounded souls is to thoroughly engage human bodies and body politics where the soul emerges and resides.

The Soul and the *Imago Dei*

So, what then is the soul and how do we conceive its relation to God's moral architecture given to us in creation and revealed through divine love? To understand the soul, we must first be clear about what the soul is not. The key question to answer is whether the soul is a spiritual entity that lives apart from the body, or whether the soul is a creative emergent from the person's embodied participation in nature, history, and culture. If we conclude that the soul is indeed separate from the body, time, and history then to treat wounded souls requires us to marginalize, constrain, or even deny the body. Soul repair in this mode would involve an empowering disconnection of the soul from the injuring and disempowering environment, including the bodily environment temporarily housing the soul.

But, if the soul is regarded as integral dimension of the totality of the person in the world, including the world of one's own body, then there is no retreat from the body in the turn to the morally injured soul and the spiritually burdened psyche. In this view, the body is not the temporary housing of the soul. Rather, the life of the body in the world generates the soul's existence in the first place. The body and soul are co-creations of the person in interpersonal relations, culture, and nature. Neither body nor soul is a fixed entity, standing above or outside of one another as they go through time and history. Together they emerge and co-create one another from their moral and relational enactments intrapsychically and social-culturally.

The soul becomes injured because it is malleable and subject to influence; the soul is capable of renewal and healing because it is creative and evolving. The soul, then, is a dynamically emerging and changing psycho-affective gestalt constellating thought, memory, meanings, intentions, will, and desires arising from embodied interactions of the person with self, others, culture, nature, and history. The architecture of the soul is textured, comprised of historical epochs in the life experience of persons and communities. It is layered with multiple units of meaning and values, narrative memories, contextually creative endeavors, and intrusive assaults. The soul is revealed and hidden, mysterious and familiar, enduring and emerging, agential and receptive. The body and soul are, thus, contextually creative subsystems of the person working collaboratively to enhance life and heal brokenness. In some cases the soul takes the lead in relation to the body; sometimes the body calms, grounds, and enlivens the soul. But always they are together in both apparent and inexplicable ways.

All the moral challenges that this book addresses are about body and soul united together in the life of the world. Moral living is embodied living. Moral injury always has something to do with the body: its actions, desires, appearance, social location, gender, sexual orientation, race, vulnerability, capacity for violence, and its healing properties. To be in the image of God as loving and oriented toward relational justice is always a matter of the unity of soul-body-environment struggling to act in concert for contextually creative moral advances and healing from the brokenness of the bonds that unite body, soul, and environment.

So, finally, how does one connect God as a righteous moral architect characterized by love and relational justice to embodied humans on earth living morally? How does the moral machinery characterizing God become part of the moral machinery of human beings, Christian or not? The theological answer linking divine nature to human reality is the concept of the "image of God." One of the most central theological affirmations in Christianity is that humans are created in the image of God. Divine nature and human nature and destiny are forever linked through the concept of the image of God, or the *imago Dei*. What it means to be created in the "image of God" has been interpreted in many ways. In this book, *imago Dei* refers to the capacity of human beings to, like God, engage in contextually creative loving and just relationships through which to empower vital personal, communal, and ecophilial living. God is more than a moral architect. God is also a contextually creative moral agent whose presence in the universe makes it possible for humans in the image of God to be moral builders as well. If God is a moral architect and moral agent, so also are humans created in the *imago Dei*. It is part of our moral machinery. These capacities are not optional; they are given with our nature and are empowered by God who works with and through us to bring about increased embodiments of love, relational justice, and ecological vitality.

God as Moral Challenge

The above discussion indicates that some of the dominant implications following from the traditional idea of God are open to positive and helpful interpretations for enhancing life. But already we have seen that some dimensions of this traditional idea raise questions and beg for revision, such as our understanding of the body and soul connection. These are not the only challenges the classical idea of God presents when it comes to moral matters. For not only has God been regarded as loving and just in Christianity (and other monotheistic cultures), God has often been viewed in classical Christian theology as the all-powerful and righteous Lord of History. God may seem benign when thought of as loving and redemptive. However, when justice is tied to notions of divine wrath and punishment for wrongdoing, moral dissonance becomes a central issue. This is not an easy issue to address in pastoral work with persons who are struggling with moral concerns. Living on the axis of forgiveness versus punishment is a huge moral challenge because of the teachings many of us have inherited about God's love versus God's wrath. Theologies in which omnipotence and judgment play central roles raise profound issues for responding to moral stress, dissonance, and injury.

So, what is the problem with the idea of God as the omnipotent, just, and loving moral center of history and nature? First, there is the problem that if there is one God in the universe how come there are so many diverse moral codes on earth including non-theistic ones? If they all ultimately derive from the one true God how do we understand this diversity and adjudicate these differences? Much of the moral conflict in the world is from monotheists who set their moral compasses differently from other monotheistic standpoints. Whose compass should determine the compass for everyone else? What are our moral obligations to those whose compasses lead them on a different, sometimes offensive, course with respect to our own? Incredible moral dissonance and injury have resulted from the way humans have fought about and organized their relationships to one another around conflicting moral codes derived from monotheistic-centered frameworks.

Second, there is the age-old theodicy question. If God is all-powerful and Lord of History, how come there is sin, moral evil, and moral injury in the world? Could not God prevent this? If whatever happens is ultimately by the will of God, does this mean human freedom, contextual creativity, and human moral responsibilities are fine illusions but a waste of spiritual and social energy? Should we have faith that God will resolve all moral conflicts in the long run? I have found in my work that, in fact, many persons do overcome these questions and feelings of dissonance by trusting God to harmonize power and love and by believing God has some purpose unknown to us. This allows them to assume a loving presence that sustains, renews, and transforms their lives in the face of dissonance and injury. It offers sufferers of moral injury, both victims and perpetrators, something more than a sense of divine abandonment or punishment. So in the face of dissonance and injury, many persons still find sustenance, meaning, and hope in the classical idea of God.

But if this more benign permutation on the classical idea of God helps some in the face of dissonance and injury, there remains for many a more terrifying and morally problematic version of God's power and its relation to our moral actions. God is Lawgiver and Judge. For some, the message of the tradition has been that if we obey the divine law given to God's people or embedded in our hearts by God, we will receive blessing. Our lives will be full and rich. If we forsake these obligations, bad things will happen, both as a natural consequence and as divine punishment. Because of these views of God, it is not uncommon to ask when something goes wrong, "What did I do to deserve this? What is God trying to teach me through this mess? Am I beyond redemption?" Where notions of God as Judge are operative, much of the pastoral care and spiritual guidance for persons in crisis orients itself around questions of divine intentions and the moral corrections that might be required to set things right. These questions present enormous challenges but even here many still find a foundation for healing souls by continuing to wed divine power firmly to divine love in the face of the need for moral accountability and moral correction.

But such a resolution is not always possible in relation to the traditional idea of God. What happens when there is no way that I can conceive that the bad things happening to me are deserved by my actions? Think of Job. He did not accept his friends' judgment that his adversity was punishment for moral flaws or failure on his part. Most readers of Job probably concur with Job's judgment on this score. His was undeserved suffering. Did this come from God, the all-powerful Lord of History? From God the all-loving? From the God of justice? How could anyone think that what God allowed to happen to Job was loving and just? The pastor and spiritual care provider's office is filled with stories of anguish, guilt, and defiance toward the experience of undeserved suffering by those who have been morally injured by the unchecked violence of others. Where is God in this? How do I reset my moral compass with or without God when God either caused or did not prevent undeserved harm from happening to me? The moral judgment begins to turn against God instead of humans; the gyroscope wobbles.

Another permutation on this interrogation of the traditional God has been to suggest there is a moral duality in God. God is both creator of the good and its destroyer. Some say that Job's righteousness was ultimately made possible by God's benevolent goodness as rewarder of virtue and sustainer of Job's life in the midst of grievous adversity. Others contend the all-powerful God has given us free will that accounts for tragedy and injury. Still others suggest that God could indeed be regarded as Job's enemy who callously made a bet with Satan to undeservedly inflict Job's life with bad things. What kind of God blesses first, then destroys, then blesses again? Amy Erickson and Walter Brueggemann, two well-respected biblical scholars, have argued that indeed the ambiguity of God as just and unjust is built into the monotheistic tradition and cannot be escaped.[5] This is the case for Jews and Christians alike. The God of the Jesus on the cross is the God of Job. Many persons embrace these seeming ambiguities, trying to live creatively and morally within the tensions of their religious tradition. But for many others today, the moral, existential, and intellectual implications of the dominant idea of God have become unacceptable. The spiritual and moral task of caregivers, therefore, is to understand that some who leave their monotheistic traditions may do so because they cannot abide such implications and do not intend to waste their spiritual capital trying to accommodate the moral injury that such a view has engendered in them. Though the monotheistic moral gyroscope still holds for some, it in fact wobbles or has fallen over for many others.

Finally, this book wants to suggest that alternatives have emerged in Christian theology that provide different emphases and directions than do the various expressions of classical theology. These alternatives provide ways through the moral and intellectual challenges to classical ideas of God. I think there is a steadier gyroscope available to us. Just as process, feminist, and liberation theologies suggested new ways of understanding our human selfhood not as isolated and independent but as social and interdependent, so, too, do these theologies offer creative ideas of God that may be helpful in the context of moral injury and moral dissonance. They offer radical revisioning of our understanding of God's relation to moral evil and human suffering. In particular, process and feminist theology challenged the notions of an omnipotent and unchanging God, uninvolved and independent from the world. From these two perspectives, ideas of omnipotence and unengaged transcendence are both intellectually incomprehensible and morally reprehensible. For many feminists and process thinkers, the universe is not controlled by one omnipotent agent but consists of a multiplicity of finite realities that both are agents and recipients of others' actions. In this view, God is a creative participant who has more power than all other agents but does not have all power. Rather than God being the controller of all that occurs, blessing and injury alike, God is the creativity in the universe that makes change and transformation possible. Other realities, including humans, contribute to the direction of life. All of reality, including divine and human, are thus part of an interdependent process rather than a one directional movement of power. In this broadly conceived alternative to classical theology, God indeed acts redemptively for the sake of moral advances, seeking in every context the best possible outcomes given the circumstances. God does not cause moral darkness, but is the source of the light and sustaining power that rises in the darkness. Here God is in solidarity with us in our moral struggles and suffering, not their omnipotent cause. Moral failures are the complex outcomes of multiple forces that God seeks to reconcile and stimulate for the highest possible good. Moral guidance in this view requires pastoral and spiritual caregivers to realistically assess the responsible agencies accounting for the moral dissonances, dilemmas, and injuries with an eye to amelioration and healing. God, in this perspective, is conceived as an agent of preserving, awakening, and renewing life after moral demises. Rather than being the direct or indirect cause of all good and evil in the world, God is a partner in the struggle for a more just world with less pain and more creative possibilities for all.

The main takeaway for this volume is that the pastor as moral guide cannot too easily assume that discourse about God's relation to the moral challenges on the table will be met with an unambiguous welcome. An individual's experience in relation to faith and theology may in fact disqualify the pastor as a moral authority, especially if the person seeking counsel believes that God is responsible by action or inaction for their moral predicaments, or that a sense of God as condemning Judge is more spiritually powerful than a sense of God as loving, forgiving, and transforming.

Moral discernment requires theological assessment. Collaborative conversation about the religious and theological ideals that are functioning for individuals and groups in the moral situation is an important and fruitful way to proceed. It helps, without judgment or expectation, to safely explore what operative views of God are actually relevant to the moral challenges being considered. Learning together through exploratory mutual conversation is a better way to proceed rather than the caregiver plunking his or her normative assumptions about God into the matrix with the expectation that they will (1) be received positively, (2) be relevant to the operative theologies of the parties, and (3) be useful resources for healing. In most cases, a viable view of God's moral relevance to the careseeker's situation must be discovered and fashioned (or refashioned) as an outcome of the collaborative process rather than as its starting point. In any case, it is essential that the pastor and spiritual caregiver recognize, with Brueggemann, that there are many "theodicy settlements" operating in scripture, tradition, theology, and experience.[6] Because God's relation to evil is itself a moral matter, any pastoral guidance with respect to God, moral failure, and moral healing must take account of the diverse theodicy settlements that may be layered into the moral injury under consideration.

Strategic Example—God: My Moral Enemy

Mrs. Burkett's soul was grievously wounded after she lost her child and her husband abandoned their family and his Christian faith. She sought spiritual counsel for the tormenting pain she was trying to manage.[7] Mr. Burkett's parents had been religious leaders in a context of urban violence in the United States. They were severely injured in the course of their duties and remained in ill health afterwards. Further, due to conflicts between them and the organization sponsoring their ministry they lost their home and livelihood and barely eked out a living. This was very difficult for the family, and for Mr. Burkett as a young man. Nonetheless, he was driven by a passion to continue the work of his parents on behalf of social justice. He married a woman who shared this commitment. He and Mrs. Burkett indeed affiliated with community organizing and advocacy groups. They served with appreciation and felt they were blessed by God to be in this ministry. Then their youngest child contracted a disease and suddenly died. They were devastated. They could not continue their ministry. Their marriage and their family fell apart. They had to find a way to hold themselves together, heal, and move on.

At the heart of their moral crisis were their respective views of God's goodness. She believed that God was good no matter what happened. She did not attribute what happened to Mr. Burkett's parents or their son to an act of God. She attributed these events to the risks of living in a fragile world where undeserved bad things can happen to genuinely good people. She found consolation in her faith and strength from God through her family, friends, and church.

Mr. Burkett, however, attributed his losses to the cruel hand of God. "I did not deserve this. My family does not deserve this. We answered God's call to serve him. God promised us blessing and protection if we followed in his way. We did nothing wrong. We followed in his way. It was too much that God would let these bad things happen to my parents. But that God would take my son is totally unacceptable. I will defy this God for the rest of my life. He does not deserve my devotion any longer."

In the face of their horrendous losses, God is the central moral issue for the Burketts. Mr. Burkett blames God for not keeping his promise to bless and protect. God took too much and gave too little. This loss shattered Mr. Burkett's moral compass. When he reset his compass, his new orientation led him away from his moral commitments to his marriage and family, and to his own personal health and welfare. He lived carelessly, driven by protest and defiance against God the Unfaithful. He does not, at this point in time, have another way to move theologically, personally, and relationally. God has become his enemy, without access to the other side of God, either as preserver of life or as comforter in affliction. His moral injury is too great to sustain or consider other possibilities.

For Mrs. Burkett, God is an ally. She finds comfort in God and nurture from her faith community. She does not attribute bad things to a good God. Her moral compass is intact, but she is devastated by the consequences of her husband's theological and moral injuries. Her main moral challenge is to decide whether (and how) to move on, or not. She does not want a divorce but cannot see an alternative to his determination to leave behind everything that he received from his former moral bargain with God, his family, and his religious community. Mrs. Burkett struggles with a moral dilemma. Should she let him go, trust him to God, and keep the door open for what may change down the line? Or should she hold on tighter, standing faithfully on the promise of their lifelong moral commitments to their marriage vows, trusting the goodness of God and her husband's capacity for healing? In any case, she has no intention of keeping him from their other two children. This moral dilemma was difficult for her. Because of pressures from her husband and his lawyer, she felt she had to accede to a divorce. But she also made it clear that the door was open for engagement with him and access to the children so long as he was not exposing them to destructive behaviors or dangerous environments.[8]

I present this strategic example to illustrate that views of God are (1) endemic in moral challenges, (2) often dissonant and are sources of moral dilemmas and even moral injuries, and (3) do not always lead to positive outcomes for all the parties. Some moral challenges and injuries are simply too big and too complex for healing to come about in a straightforward or timely manner. Grieving losses and learning to live with what is "left over" is sometimes the most we can embrace as a caregiving outcome.

Habits of Mind Exercise

Before concluding the discussion of God and moral injury, I would like to turn the reader to a brief habits of mind exercise. Using a journal, please identify your inner dialogue as you read these sections. What excited you? What were you curious about? What challenged you? If possible, name a moral issue that you are struggling with. Describe its core features. Identify how you believe God is related to this issue. How is your inner dialogue about your moral issue affected when you introduce the idea of God into it? How might your ideas of God be a part of the moral injury itself? How might some of the "theodicy settlements" you read about above change the frame in more benevolent or actionable terms for you? What complications would changing the frame bring about? In taking action to address your views of God, how might you pray at this point in time? What outcomes would you pray for? If God is in some way responsible for your moral injury, how would you best protest this? Is forgiveness of God a possibility to consider? How might your actions and your reframing influence a revision of your views of God? Do you need to revise your theology to heal from your moral injury? Who can help you with this? What steps can you take? What other conclusions or questions do you have before moving on? How has this exercise benefitted you? What will you keep from it?

For Further Reading

Farley, Wendy. *Tragic Vision and Divine Compassion: A Contemporary Theodicy.* Louisville: Westminster John Knox, 1990.

Gebara, Ivone. *Out of the Depths: Women's Experience of Evil and Salvation.* Minneapolis: Fortress, 2002.

Keller, Catherine. *On the Mystery: Discerning Divinity in Process.* Minneapolis: Fortress, 2008.

Kushner, Harold S. *When Bad Things Happen to Good People: With a New Preface by the Author.* New York: Schocken Books, 2001.

Nelson, Susan L. "Facing Evil: Evil's Many Faces." *Interpretation* 57, no. 4 (2003): 398–413.

CHAPTER 6

Dissonance and Dilemmas

Moral dissonance is the natural and normal condition of our lives and ministries. Embracing moral dissonance and moral dilemmas as normal and natural is the first step to handling them creatively. Moral dissonances generate moral dilemmas. A skillful embrace of the palpable dissonances and dilemmas coursing through our spirits and relationships may lead to moral advances for persons and communities. As we saw in the case of Pastor Lawson in chapter 4, sensitive handling of moral dissonance and dilemmas can prevent moral injury. At the same time, we will see that morally injured persons live with complicated moral dissonance and often generate difficult moral dilemmas for themselves and others.

How do we as ministers help ourselves and those we serve to live well in the vast kaleidoscopic landscape of conflicting moral options and pressing moral dilemmas that demand a response? I find the concept of "contextual creativity" to be a basis for acting as vital agents in responding well to the moral dilemmas we actually face. Contextual creativity is the capacity to receive with appreciation the concrete circumstances that make up the dissonances and dilemmas of our lives—our contexts—and to imaginatively respond with creative alternatives. Contextual creativity recognizes the social and relational "givenness" of things, but also acknowledges that reality is in flux and that we can shape what life will be through our engagement with the dilemmas confronting us. Put simply, contextual creativity means that "where there is life, there is hope." Contextual creativity means that change is always possible, no matter what the circumstances, even though the change that is possible may not be readily apparent, immediate, or unduly large.

But, contextual creativity is not uncontested or uncomplicated. Not only does it respond to dissonance and dilemmas, it may be the cause of dissonance and moral conflict. The past pulls us to conformity. The present threatens to constrict us. The future can be too open or too closed to guide us. There is something scary as well as something promising in the potential we hold to be creative in response to the pressures and opportunities afforded to us in our particular contexts. However, when linked to the moral pillars of naming, framing, enacting, and revising, contextual creativity can become a habit of mind through which we may genuinely revitalize our lives. In this chapter I provide examples of dissonance, dilemmas, and contextual creativity along with strategic examples of moral advances made possible by collaborative engagement.

Warring Moral Tribes

Moral living takes place in specific times and places and is conducted by individuals and groups who are ferociously committed to fulfilling their obligations to what they believe is necessary for their survival and well-being. To be morally intact, communities must resolve internal moral dissonance and protect themselves from the moral hegemony of outsiders. Moral living is inherently contentious; it puts individuals and groups into unalterable conflict. Life is fraught with moral dissonance arising from conflicted moral communities, or moral tribes. How do we account for this and manage it in our commitment to find healthy collaborations in the face of destructive potentials?

Moral psychology is a research field that can be employed to address moral dissonance and contribute to healing from moral injury. Moral psychology assists us in understanding the diverse frames, foundations, and factors inherent in moral decision-making. It is particularly helpful for understanding sympathetically why good people set their moral compasses in opposite directions from one another. Moral psychologists, like Jonathan Haidt, have been influential contributors to my work on moral dissonance, injury, and healing. They make it very plain that our moral gyroscopes indeed wobble, and help to explain why.

Moral psychologists demonstrate that to live morally, which is broadly defined as regulating one's self-interest in order to favorably enhance the larger welfare of one's kin and primary groupings, is a binding social process that protects one's social group against threat from outsiders and regulates cooperative processes internal to one's own group.[1] Moral living, by nature, unites and excludes; it "binds and blinds," in Haidt's terms.[2] It is primarily a pre-rational process, though rational judgments are brought to bear at strategic points to resolve dissonance and to take account of the welfare of outsiders.[3] Moral living is an encultured emotional process generated and advanced by linking individual moral intuitions to public rituals, practices, and everyday immersion in the complex array of relationships we have in the world. Moral psychologists theorize precognitive, rational, and ideological factors in relation to the immediacy of life in particular social groups.[4]

However, moral psychologists do not operate out of the same view of human community as I am proposing. They emphasize the construction and maintenance of moral narratives in distinct social groups. I have argued for a comprehensive panhuman anthropology that both affirms particular uniqueness and recognizes that human welfare requires relational justice across "all our relations." Nonetheless, moral psychologists are quite useful to help us understand how moral compasses as well as moral dissonances come into being and how they might be modified through collaborative processes. Moral psychology offers us three particular resources. The first is the notion of moral foundations and moral matrices. The second is the notion of moral tribes. The third is the identification of moral narratives. Together these three elements provide a keen understanding of the moral machinery underlying moral dissonance, dilemmas, injury, and healing. I will present them in combination, rather than separately in the text to follow.

Haidt identifies six moral foundations, or axes, that might be combined to form a range of moral orientations.[5] These can stand alone, but most commonly are configured into somewhat fixed patterns for individuals and cultures. These foundations, under the press of nature, history, culture, and psychology, become the basis for the creation of enduring moral matrices for individuals and groups. That is, they set the directions of the moral compass to be followed by "tribes" clustering around the moral narratives growing out of particular combinations of the moral frames or moral foundations available to us.

The six moral foundations are

- care/harm

- liberty/oppression

- fairness/cheating

- loyalty/betrayal

- authority/subversion

- sanctity/degradation

Social liberals constitute a tribe or recognizable grouping that orients its moral compass by favoring care over harm, liberty over oppression, and fairness and justice over cheating and social inequality. They put less emphasis upon loyalty to a community or organization, deference to authority, and maintaining sanctity or purity of one's primary reference groups. In fact, the moral narrative of the liberal tribe identifies the conservative's moral foundations as the core moral problem to overcome through care, justice, and liberation. Conservatives, as viewed by liberals, regard loyalty to the established order and to one's primary groupings, obedience to authority, and exclusion of "the other" in order to maintain group purity as the foundation for the morally flawed policies and practices that that make liberation, fairness, justice, and care necessary in the first place. That is to say, for the social liberal, the way that social conservatives in the United States apply their moral foundations is the main reason the body politic and many groups and individuals within it become morally injured.

The moral foundations favored by social conservatives, according to Haidt, are more comprehensive than those emphasized by social liberals. Social conservatives indeed prize loyalty to a group and obedience to authority over individual autonomy and critical thinking. In fact, they are deeply concerned in maintaining the identity and viability of their primary groups and organizations by clearly defining and limiting access to outsiders. But, in addition, they organize themselves to extend care and promote justice for their own, and secure freedom from oppression, pollution, or invasion by outsiders. Haidt argues that because the moral foundations are more comprehensive for conservatives, and that they prize group cohesion over individual rights and multicultural belonging, they have stronger social capital in the long haul. That is, according to this theory, the more limited moral foundations comprising the liberal narrative run a greater danger of undermining capacities necessary for establishing the society they are trying to create. Without attention to obedience, loyalty, and boundary markers, unrestrained individualism and chaotic social consequences are nearly inevitable. Conversely, the danger for social conservatives is to create a nondemocratic authoritarian structure that privileges the established order, limits the strengths that can come from diversity, and perpetuates various social and economic inequalities.

The 2016 presidential election in the United States reflected the polarities of social liberal and social conservative moral narratives. Those supporting the Democratic candidate, Hillary Clinton, forcefully emphasized the value of a diverse rather than rigidly bounded nation and promoted policies that support those most marginalized by the oppressions of racism, sexism, and heterosexism. The Democrats question established authorities and tilt the structures of government and civic life to include religious diversity and economic fairness, and to correct the injustices of history. They want to conserve social programs such as affordable healthcare and women's right to have access to contraceptives and abortion, and to strengthen Medicare, Medicaid, and Social Security. They are committed to the full rights of citizenship of women and sexual minorities such as gays, lesbians, and transgendered persons. Democrats want to strengthen public health and safety through meaningful gun safety laws and various regulations to ensure justice and accountability in the marketplace. They are committed to protecting and healing the environment from various ecological threats.

The conservative moral narrative of the Republican Party and its current leader, Donald J. Trump, are incensed with how the nation is, in their view, crime-ridden and economically vulnerable. These social conservatives want to "make America great again" by limiting access to outsiders and returning undocumented foreigners to their homelands. They believe that governmental regulations and tax and spending policies have become oppressive, leading to great injustice for many workers and their families. They want to pull back from trade agreements and security alliances, and to redefine America's unique place in the global order. They believe that our many entitlement programs undermine rather than strengthen the social order. They are opposed to the injustice of the present tax code, especially how much the American taxpayer is unfairly being asked to support unjust causes and unworthy recipients. They believe that attempts to regulate the environment, finance, and gun safety represent oppressive government overreach. And they oppose laws in favor of contraception, abortion, racial justice, and sexual diversity. All of these social goods prized by liberals are seen by conservatives as undermining rather than strengthening the social fabric that has made and that will "make America great again."

I present these metanarratives comprising the moral landscape of the United States in the second decade of the twenty-first century to underscore how moral dissonance, moral dilemmas, moral injury, and moral healing come about through the processes of history and culture. Good people have moral compasses where True North leads in different directions! In Haidt's words,

> Morality binds and blinds. It binds us into ideological teams that fight each other as though the fate of the world depended on our side winning each battle. It blinds us to the fact that each team is composed of good people that have something important to say.[6]

This "binding and blinding" has eventuated in moral dissonances that are not readily harmonized at this time in American history. Not only do we have wobbly moral compasses, but some are in a moral fight to the death with one another. Our moral binding and blinding are currently sources of great moral conflict and significant moral injury in our interpersonal relationships and body politic. Religious communities are part and parcel of this moral cauldron, and in fact contribute to it by the dissonant moral narratives that have grown up within religious bodies and leaked into the public square over the centuries.[7]

Is there a way through or beyond this escalating polarity? Haidt's conclusions are fairly vague and preliminary. He is realistic about how polarization has deepened and is self-perpetuated by a win-lose mentality that prevents compromise. However, he also knows that these positions have emerged in time and history to address various challenges and, therefore, they are in principle modifiable under changing historical circumstances. Haidt believes that we can move from a warlike winner-take-all to a more yin and yang harmony of differences by expanding our moral intuitions through greater human contact with our moral adversaries. He asks us to take intentional steps toward a genuine understanding of what is morally sacred to one another in particular moral issues:

> And if you really want to open your mind, open your heart first. If you can have at least one friendly interaction with a member of the "other" group, you will find it far easier to listen to what they're saying, and maybe even see a controversial issue in a new light.[8]

Haidt's invitation to open hearts through "friendly interaction" is akin to my emphasis upon authentic collaborative engagement as moral equals with curious openness to listen, understand, and discover. Rather than conceiving one another as enemies, it invites us to consider that "I am as we are." It reflects Mucherera's teachings about Palaver. This is a tall order in our current church and society. It may be a fool's errand. And it certainly cannot be conceived as the only way to progress. Before we can come together we may find ourselves fracturing beyond recognition and building something beyond the grasp or aspiration of the current polarities. Indeed, we know from astute social scientific research that social systems are subject to schizmogenesis, or the tendency to split apart because of escalating conflict.[9] However, it is also possible for parties to emerge in conflicted social systems that modify the pressures for splitting and find fruitful possibilities for compromise without capitulation. Reframing the conflict in terms of both subgroup and mega-group success can go a long way toward fashioning a contextually creative basis for moral advance. As this book proceeds, the reader will be presented with various strategies of collaborative engagement to minimize moral dissonance, to resolve moral dilemmas, and to prevent as well as heal from the moral injuries fomented by our style of moral discourse.

To summarize and conclude, history and culture provide a massive array of resources by which to set our moral compasses and to preserve our identities as we find our way within the cosmos and with one another. We have been given an elaborate mixture of precedents and practices by which to set our course and to correct it as we go. But these macrosystemic moral gyroscopes are wobbly and conflicted. Thus, we have no choice but to become contextually creative in how we regard and incorporate what we have been given in time and history, and in how we correct and repair the damages that accrue from the morally injurious legacies of the past. The core task before us now, as I conceive it, is to mitigate the warring moral orientations that threaten our welfare and continue to inflict moral injury on one another.

In the remainder of this chapter, I want to highlight four strategic examples of how moral dissonance and moral dilemmas appear in a wide variety of contexts in order to assist the reader to engage collaboratively parallel situations in their own lives and ministries. I will also introduce a mental exercise to assist with gaining clarity about responding creatively to moral challenges.

After you have read each of these examples, take time for a brief habits of mind exercise. What excites and interests you about this account? What challenges you? When you consider situations like this in your life or ministry, how did you negotiate them? How might reading about these experiences contribute insights to moral conundrums with which you are dealing? What kind of collaborative conversation do you imagine? What kind of moral courage may be required in your circumstances?

Strategic Example: Pastor Gregory's Jailhouse Conundrum

A pastoral colleague shared a compelling dilemma from his ministry. He was caught between dissonant moral compasses in a complex correctional facility. His contextually creative responses are instructive. He has given permission to use this vignette. His identity is anonymous.

Pastor Gregory, a Protestant minister, was senior minister in a New England parish that was located next door to the county jail. He became the part-time chaplain and developed strong relationships with the county sheriff who oversaw the jail. He became close to many of the prisoners. He was highly respected and was called upon to provide care and guidance in many situations.

Pastor Gregory realized that there was a high suicide risk among inmates, and he initiated a suicide-prevention program, which involved training some of the inmates to be helpful responders to other prisoners who might be at risk. One of the prisoners who took the class was an notable man with whom Pastor Gregory developed a particularly close bond. "I really respected him. Let's call him Julio, though that is not his name. Julio was smart, strong, and a natural leader. He was very eager to take my course and to help others who might need him. Because he was involved, other prisoners also took part. When I would go to the jail I would always talk with Julio; we really 'got' each other."

Pastor Gregory expressed to the sheriff how impressed he was with Julio. The sheriff said, "You ought to be impressed with him. After all, he runs the prison. I may be the sheriff, but nothing happens there without Julio's knowledge and permission. He keeps things in line. He takes care of the prisoners when they need help, and he makes sure that they know he is the boss and that he runs things inside." Pastor

Gregory was not surprised to learn this, based on his sense of Julio's personal charisma and authority.

One day, a young inmate came to Pastor Gregory in acute distress. "Let's call him Manuel. Manuel was all shaken up because he knew he has done something wrong—he had broken the rules Julio had set—and he was going to be punished for it. He knew he had done wrong and he knew that he was going to get what he deserved. He was really scared. He said, 'Can you talk to Julio for me? I know he trusts you.' I was in a bind. I couldn't ask Julio to break the rules, because if Julio didn't uphold the rules he would have lost his authority. And I did not want to weaken my relationship with Julio. On the other hand, I didn't want this young man to be hurt. He wasn't going to be killed, but he definitely was going to be hurt to teach him a lesson for what he did."

Pastor Gregory decided to build on his relationship with Julio to intercede for Manuel, but to do so in a way that maintained the prison hierarchy and strengthen Julio's role at the top. "I went to Julio and said, 'Julio, I am here to ask you to do something. I know that Manuel broke the rules and deserves to be punished, but I am going to ask you—just this once—to have mercy on him and not to harm him. I am asking you to do this; Manuel isn't. So, as a favor to me, I am requesting you not to harm him.'"

Julio's response was predictable. "I can't do that, man. I will lose my authority and after that no one will respect me. There won't be any order in here."

Pastor Gregory said, "Not necessarily. Actually, if you show mercy this one time, and make it clear that it is your choice to do this because I asked you to—and it is only for one time!—then it will strengthen your authority. They will know that you have the strength to choose mercy as well as inflict punishment. That will give you more power rather than less in their eyes. And you can be sure that I won't intervene again for Manuel or anyone else who breaks the rules."

Julio accepted Pastor Gregory's request. He didn't ask for any favors in return. No one else came to Pastor Gregory to speak with Julio on their behalf. As far as Pastor Gregory knows, nothing negative came out of this for Manuel, who avoided pain and injury because Julio chose mercy over punishment this one time.

In reflecting on this situation, several features stand out, and some questions come to mind. What stands out is the moral ambiguity about what is "the right thing" to do in the face of moral dissonance between several "micro-moral" systems at work. Pastor Gregory had to negotiate his role in the prisoner subsystem as a whole, with his personal and pastoral relationship to Julio, his accountability to the sheriff and the judicial system, and his pastoral relationship to Manuel. In the final analysis, Pastor Gregory's actions were determined by his pastoral relationship to Manuel, but were enacted in a complex network of intersecting dissonant moral codes. Failure to negotiate this precarious moral landscape with respect and sensitivity could have had disastrous consequences, including being implicated in illegal acts of violence against an inmate.

Second, Pastor Gregory's moral actions were based upon genuine respect and trust between him and the other powerful players in this moral context. He had strong bonds with Julio and did not challenge the moral subsystem over which Julio had control. He had tacit support from the sheriff to recognize, maintain, and work with Julio's authority. And he had a pastoral commitment to Manuel's vulnerability and well-being, without colluding with illegal acts against him. This was a morally risky situation, mitigated by trust and open collaboration with all the players active in this challenging dilemma.

In terms of the moral landscape, Pastor Gregory was not a passive reactor, but contributed to a moral advance through reframing power in terms of choice and mercy. He was contextually creative in a constrictive moral climate. Before Pastor Gregory's intervention, Julio, Manuel, and the inmate hierarchy saw power and obedience to the moral codes in hierarchical and retributive terms. Authority was maintained by dispensing punishment for wrongdoing through the threat or application of violent action. In this context, the most violent actor is the most authoritative actor, and morality becomes a matter of obedience, mediated by fear and violence. Indeed, this is the master narrative organizing the power and values of the prison system as a whole, including the prisoner subsystem. Pastor Gregory offered another way of interpreting and enacting power: the capacity to choose mercy and the wisdom to interpret mercy as strength. And though the strength of mercy was ultimately made credible in the jail population by threat of future physical punishment, for the moment, in this situation, power was redefined, enacted creatively, and the moral authority of the actor was enhanced.

Where did Pastor Gregory get this capacity? As far as I know, he did not go to a case conference, clergy support group, staff consultation, or prison chaplain handbook. There was something inherent in the concrete relationships in the prison intersecting his moral compass that led to spontaneously creative moral action. He proceeded collaboratively and openly with the other actors, joining their self-interest to his values as a resource for expanding moral choices. He utilized his considerable personal integrity, theological grounding, and moral agency to respect the personhood and integrity of others, and to expand moral agency for all the other parties. "I simply went with the flow, following the path that 'felt' right, feeling my way through this to try to get a win/win outcome."

Certainly, other options were available. He could have consulted with the sheriff for his wisdom and guidance as a part of his primary accountability. He could have left it to the sheriff to protect Manuel within the policies and codes of the correctional system. Did Pastor Gregory's joining Julio's hierarchy compromise the sheriff's authority as well as his own as the community's agents with incarcerated prisoners?

Had the situation turned out badly for Manuel, would Pastor Gregory have colluded with the wrong moral code in this situation?

Another option was for Pastor Gregory to challenge the dominant moral discourse from a different standpoint. Rather than maintaining and reframing Julio's hierarchical position, he might have challenged Julio's authority by putting him on notice that he had information that would implicate Julio in any harm done to Manuel. Rather than joining Julio's prisoner subsystem, he would have challenged or destabilized it by a threatening appeal to a higher accountability. Had he taken this course, Pastor Gregory would have (1) played into the hierarchy that threat of harm rather than mercy was the operative norm, (2) lost his status and bond with Julio, and (3) most likely contributed to physical injury to Manuel.

Or Pastor Gregory might have challenged Julio's moral position by inviting him to consider a radically different way of organizing his life and structuring his relationships to others. He might have suggested that violence-secured hierarchical power was a losing game, and that this was a good time for Julio to think of other alternatives and to begin to practice them with pastoral guidance and support. Had Pastor Gregory taken this course, perhaps Julio would have grown into a servant-leader in jail and after release. But there would also be an acute risk of Julio rejecting this overture, cancelling their bond, and reasserting his power in harsh terms against Manuel.

Moral cultures clash in any context where moral action is called for. There are usually multiple options for action, or inaction, but dissonance may coalesce into an unavoidable focused dilemma as it did for Pastor Gregory. No matter what action is chosen or not chosen, there are potentially dangerous or unhappy (and unintended) consequences. Pastor Gregory was astute, lucky, and effective in terms of this specific event. Its impact down the road on Julio, jail culture, and Manuel's growth is unknown. But there is usually a modicum of insufficiency in all our moral actions, even when they also contribute to some degree of moral advance. As Luther would have it, we are *simul justes et peccator*, sinners and saints alike: always, in all actions and inactions.

Strategic Example: Collaborative Chaplaincy End-of-Life Decision

Diverse moral gyroscopes arising from nature, culture, and history combine to present us with complex moral challenges. They also may co-contrive to fashion contextually creative moral advances from their richness. Chaplain Jamie Beachy offers a gripping account of an end-of-life decision that required sensitive collaborative engagement of culturally diverse and morally dissonant values in an acute hospital setting. What follows is summarized and edited from her PhD dissertation.[10]

Mrs. V. is a patient is on life support for injuries sustained in a bicycle-car acci-
dent. She is originally from Bangladesh, but has lived in the United States for twenty
years. She has two sons who provide loving attention to her. This is a Hindu family,
though the sons do not practice. Mrs. V. is a devout follower and practitioner of her
faith. While the doctors see her "non-responsiveness" as a sign of brain damage, her
sons interpret her calmness "as a reflection of her deep spiritual practice gained after
years of practicing yoga."

The medical team is frustrated that Mrs. V.'s sons do not support their recom-
mendation to remove her from life support. They want the student-chaplain, Mr.
L., to intervene with the family. He is a thirty-six-year-old white male Presbyterian
seminary student from an affluent urban family in the Midwest. He agrees with
the medical team and is "upset with Mrs. V.'s family because they 'cannot accept
that Mrs. V. is suffering and should be allowed to be withdrawn from the ventila-
tor' and 'allowed to die peacefully' rather than linger indefinitely in a marginally
conscious state."

Mr. L. is caught in a dissonant situation: he sides with the medical team and
seeks help from his chaplain supervisor for guidance to help convince the family to
withdraw life support. Chaplain Beachy suggests that they "go to visit Mrs. V.'s room
together to talk with the team, meet her family, and assess the situation. Mr. L. agrees
to co-collaborate on this case for the benefit of his learning."

When they arrive, the sons are in the room. They learn from the sons how important her religious practice is to Mrs. V. They share with the sons that the medical
team believes it is time to discontinue life support. The sons cannot understand why
the medical team thinks their mother is unresponsive.

> One of the sons leans down to his mother's ear and speaks gently, loudly,
> and with great tenderness in Bengali. Though Mr. L. and I do not under-
> stand the content of his words, Mrs. V.'s son's affect is deeply loving and
> intimate. Mrs. V. begins to smile and laugh. She opens one of her eyes and
> looks directly at Mr. L., who is standing beside her, and she smiles. We let
> Mrs. V.'s sons know we will help mediate the conversation between them
> and the medical team. We offer words of support to Mrs. V. and her sons
> and encourage them to bring images of Mrs. V.'s spiritual teacher into the
> hospital room for support if they feel that she would want an altar set up
> in the hospital room. We let the team know that Mrs. V. was responsive in
> her conversation with us and recommend that she only be assessed in her
> own language with her sons present. We document her sons' perspective on
> their mother's "non-responsiveness." After several months of rehabilitation,
> Mrs. V. is able to return home to live independently with some help from
> her sons.[11]

Chapter 6

The expanded conversation between the chaplains, Mrs. V. and her sons, and the medical team brought forth new knowledge and created a basis for changing the treatment plan. Cultural differences, language barriers, and dissonance between Western medical sciences and Hindu spiritual practices were bridged. They truly saw one another in new ways. They added complexity to their diagnostic categories and framed their responses in more advantageous terms. The outcome was favorable. Mr. L. was particularly able to revise his theological and pastoral approach in the light of this powerful pastoral event.

> Later in supervision, Mr. L. expresses his sense of shame and anger at his assuming that the medical team had accurately assessed Mrs. V.'s responsiveness. He is frustrated and feels embarrassed for being part of the White, male-dominated "system" that "undervalues cultural minorities." We process his experience and emotional reaction together and Mr. L. writes a theological paper on the moment that Mrs. V. "looked right at me with a depth of compassion" as a sacred and theologically significant sign of the presence of Christ for Mr. L. He writes of this moment as a turning point in his learning to become a caregiver able to rely on his own authority in his role of chaplain.[12]

I selected this powerful vignette to illustrate the complexity of moral dissonance and contextual creativity in today's interculturally sensitive healthcare chaplaincy. Chaplain Beachy found this experience to be a positive example of "creative interruption," the central metaphor that she employs to disclose the transparency and life-giving advances that can come to all parties when they are able to be authentically transparent with one another. Beachy's commitment to collaborative engagement of the patient, the patient's family, the patient's Hinduism, her CPE student, the healthcare team, her own internal process, and perspectives from Christian theology and Jewish philosopher Emmanuel Levinas disclose rich possibilities for fashioning care that led to healing and a moral advance for all the parties. Through coming into more direct contact with the "face" of the Other, and transparent visibility to one's own inner dialogues, moral dissonance gave way to creative moral advance in healing and recovery. Through naming the healthcare challenge at the end of life, reframing it in culturally sensitive and actionable terms, engaging the situation from a more collaborative standpoint, and revising self-understandings and codes of ministry, Beachy and her student, as well as the healthcare team, were able to reconstruct a culturally sensitive approach to ministry that staved off death and rekindled the powers of life in an expanded religious and human community. Macrosystemic moral gyroscopes derived from nature, history, and culture were revised in a manner that not only extended life, but that deepened and expanded the religious, moral, and intercultural codes in the protection and betterment of life.

Strategic Example: Facing a Marital Dilemma

Reverend Victoria Johnson was well-known in her conservative Baptist tradition. Bright, articulate, pastorally sensitive, and well-respected in her community for bridging racial divides, this up-and-coming African-American religious leader was troubled by a marriage that was not working. To outsiders, she and her husband were a model couple. But she knew that the marriage was sapping each of them spiritually. The dissonance between them as individuals, and the dissonance between her failing marriage and her ministry success was becoming more than she could tolerate.

When these conflicts rose to the level of crisis, they "did not seek counsel from clergy, because I was not willing. Because it was taking every inch of my being to stand against a lifetime of beliefs and core values, I knew wise counsel from clergy within the denomination or within the Black Church faith community in this local area would have put me at great risk of being seduced by the doctrines of submission and obedience. So as a matter of life or continuing to die slowly, I chose to trust and depend only on my personal and intimate relationship with God, and the spirit living within me for this life-altering, yet God movement in my life."

Her moral compass about marriage conflicted with the other side of her moral compass about relational justice: "It isn't right to stay in a marriage or any other relationship that is oppressive and harmful. I preach to others to change or leave oppressive situations. Why should that not be true for me too?" She was in agony over this dilemma. It was not apparent which direction she should take.

The time came when she could live with it no longer. A kind of "Kairos" gestalt came into place and she knew she had to divorce no matter the consequences for her ministry in her church. She knew that it would be morally wrong to continue in a harmful marriage, and morally right to end it, in spite of the threats of internal guilt and community condemnation (to use Paul Tillich's formulation). She knew she could not tolerate the moral disconnect between her oppressive marriage and her public leadership in trying to help others become liberated from oppression. So with anxiety and relief she found the courage to divorce in spite of the voices of negative judgment within and around her. She and her husband stood ready to face the next chapters in their lives.

For Rev. Johnson, the next step unfortunately turned out to be leaving her denomination. The condemnation she received for what her denomination regarded as sinful action made it impossible for her to feel that she belonged in the church that brought her to faith, called her to ministry, and cherished her leadership. So along with the decisions to leave her husband, she "also made the conscious decision to not remain a part of a faith community that did not encourage or support liberation and life to the fullest for me, and women and men equally." It was excruciating for her to lose her church and her place in it. The grief was enormous. For a while she was at sea, but not lost. She sensed God's presence in her soul and drew on the support of those closest to her.

After a time, she found her way to the United Methodist Church. The United Methodist Church welcomed her to its fellowship and ordained her to its ministry. As a Methodist minister, Rev. Johnson has become the senior minister of a multicultural suburban congregation and a leader in her community on racial justice and marriage equality. She completed her Doctor of Ministry degree and has become a mentor to many theological students discerning their vocational direction. She is now Rev. Dr. Victoria Johnson!

Rev. Dr. Johnson reflected on this life-changing decision and all that came out of it:

> I am grateful for liberation from a marriage that was robbing my life. But I didn't want to lose everything. I lost my church because of it. It hurts that the leaders in my former church didn't reach out to me after I left or show concern once I chose a different path than the one that they thought was right. To them I am a sinner who did not repent. I still feel hurt by that. But I also found something that is turning out to be much better for me. I feel at home where I am and grateful that God has led me to this place. I am healing from my divorce and from the loss of my denomination. My ministry now is full and my life is going well.

Rev. Dr. Johnson gives us a poignant window into the delicate intricacies of finding moral courage in the face of very costly moral alternatives. There was no easy way out for her. As she struggled with her dilemma, naming it clearly as a conflict between a viable marriage and a truthful ministry, she was able to reframe her options more clearly and creatively change her marriage and ministry contexts. The moral advance for Rev. Johnson was fashioning a vital congruence between her personal and professional lives. Her faith in God's goodness was deepened through God's leading her to a welcoming church and to a significant congregational and public ministry.

When we think about Rev. Dr. Johnson's story, three things come into focus. First, moral courage is the power to move beyond the fear that binds us to negative circumstances and to act in trust on the basis of what we know to be the True North on our moral compasses. For Rev. Dr. Johnson, True North meant working for liberation from oppression in all areas of her life, and not to be morally divided between her marriage and ministry. Once she knew what she had to do, the strength to move beyond her fears came into place and empowered her to engage her situation differently.

The second important insight is that when moral courage leads us from fear to freedom, it also brings with it significant loss and grief. Rev. Dr. Johnson lost a marriage to a good man and dreams of a life together. He lost his spouse and his dreams too. Her denomination lost an influential leader and a vital human being. She lost the goodwill of those who previously lauded her contributions. The pastoral care dimensions of moral courage come into focus around the emotions of fear and grief, both of which have to be borne if there is to be vital moral living. In this case, there was no ritual of grief, loss, or transition in order to have available the resources of the community for personal healing and reinvesting in life. She had to find those resources elsewhere.

The third important insight is about the nature of moral injury. Moral injury is not always about one's own moral failures and flaws. It can arise from the moral stances of others and how they present them to us. Rev. Dr. Johnson did not injure herself morally. But I believe she sustained a moral injury or moral injuries at the hands of others. Certainly, there was moral dissonance and moral dilemmas arising from the conflict in Rev. Dr. Johnson's moral commitment to relational justice in her marriage as well as in the church and society. But this dissonance and dilemma had not risen to the level of moral injury. To leave her husband was not a moral failure in her moral calculus; it was required to be true to her moral center. To be sure, she was hounded by moral tension, moral stress, and moral conflict. But she was not morally injured as far as we can tell by this conflict. But, when she became clear about what actions she needed to take to resolve her dilemmas, she was morally injured by the response of her church leaders. Her moral actions were dissonant with theirs, and they exacted the price of rejection and exile. Her moral action led to personal injury and loss that is still in the process of being healed. Put another way, sometimes our moral actions, when courageously enacted, put us in harm's way. Personal injury can be the result of acting out of our highest moral values rather than failing to embody them.

Strategic Example: The Courage to Confront a Dissonant Parish

Rev. Dr. Victoria Johnson offers another window in the dynamics of contextually creative moral courage. Moral courage came to the fore in her response to a growing dissonance between her pastoral leadership and the expectations of the multicultural suburban Methodist parish she serves as senior minister. I found her pastoral moral engagement to be particularly instructive about how love and justice can work together to bring about a moral advance in the context of ministry. In my view, Rev. Dr. Johnson's moral courage provided a bridge between love and relational justice in her parish crisis.

The parish she serves is made up of three ethnic groups: Tongans, Latinos, and Euro-Americans. The church was a large, influential Euro-American church until people moved away or passed away, leaving a small core of longtime members who think of themselves to be in charge of the parish. Into this situation came Tongans and Latinos. These three groups were not comfortable with one another. And none of them were comfortable with an African-American, womanist, social justice-oriented female pastor. "Just who I am is a moral challenge to them! There is a liberation bent in my preaching and the people do not want to hear this. They want to be a family church. They want to be cared for, not led. Many of them are military and I am not. My just showing up as an African American is to many an act of war. There is a strong tension between us. We were working together until I took a position on a social issue that they disagreed with. They said, 'The United Methodist Church doesn't deal with this.' It does, but they don't know it."

Rev. Dr. Johnson was not comfortable with them. She was frustrated by their insensitivity toward one another and their resistance toward her agenda to blend the membership into a vital whole as a justice-seeking institution in the community. Moral dissonance abounded! There was no common vision of the congregation, the groups were building resistance against one another and toward their pastor's sermons, they opposed the minister's agenda for the church, and Rev. Dr. Johnson was feeling resentment toward their relentless stubbornness. The congregation was stuck, and the pastor-parish relationship was deteriorating.

Rev. Dr. Johnson consulted with colleagues about this situation and took her concerns to God in prayer. She said, "For my own preservation I had to deal with my authentic view of the gospel that could speak to them meaningfully. My moral compass required this negotiation. Each week I had to make a decision to love these people—whether they like it or not! I had to step out of my body, take another look, and reorient myself." She realized that she was not relating to the congregation from a place of love in herself. She realized that her vision of a just and beloved community was smothering her love and respect for the actual members of her church. In fact, rather than inspiring the gospel of love and acceptance, she was embodying guilt and condemnation, which, usually has morally injurious consequences. In the name of something she envisioned as life-giving, she was participating in a congregation-wide pattern of judgmentalism toward members of her church.

Into this process came the "Charleston 9," the terrible shooting of nine people in an African-American congregation in Charleston, South Carolina, on June 17, 2015.

"I was grateful for the Charleston 9 because I could step back into the discussion of race and social justice. It reawakened our discussion of the Aurora theatre shootings [in 2012] and what should happen to James the Shooter. We were trying to find a loving response to these terrible actions. One of the Vietnam veterans in the church said, 'I was in a battle in Vietnam where 150 US soldiers were killed. But so were 2,800 Vietnamese. God loves the 2,800 Vietnamese too.'"

These events and the conversations they evoked turned her heart and mind toward the congregation in a profound way. They freed her to minister to the congregation in terms of its reality rather than in terms of her agenda. And the congregation became more responsive to the vision of love and respect for one another that she had desired. She moved from a "You should be like me" moral stance to an "I am as we are" moral stance. She and the congregation had been in oppositional moral orientation to one another. She found a way to join them in a "we-ness" that allowed them to be different while joining forces as partners rather than adversaries. There is much work to do in living this out, but it took moral courage on Rev. Dr. Johnson's part to see how she was contributing to the dissonance and moral injury that was taking place in her church and ministry. As she resolved this dilemma for herself through recognizing and feeling the love and respect that she actually held for the church, she was able to become a more efficacious moral influence in the church's life. And, since "I am as we are," the congregation could also feel the shift and become empowered by it.

Rev. Dr. Johnson's experience with her parish is a clear window into the nature of moral courage and its power to shift the moral climate of a social system such as a congregation. First, she had to recognize her lack of moral courage, even though she was linking her moral agenda to the strongest values in Christian ethics: love and justice. The way she structured love and justice in her moral economy was turning into negative attitudes toward her congregation, rather than into affirmation and respect for genuine difference. In that regard, she may have been injuring herself and others, morally speaking. Recognizing and changing this moral structure in her spirit was a courageous act of self-accountability and self-regulation. She could forgive herself and take new moral direction. She rooted her call for relational justice in a loving and respectful presence to her people. Her message and agenda did not change. But the bond to her congregation and the linkage to her own soul changed significantly. Rather than remaining in an oppositional mode to her congregation, or feeling that the moral vision and leadership for the congregation was entirely on her shoulders, she was able to join the congregation as a collaborative partner and to stand by and receive insights that arise from the experience of others.

Again, we see in Rev. Dr. Johnson's sensitive moral leadership the importance of moral courage to move us beyond anger and frustration toward ourselves and others. The pastoral leader must have the courage to recognize that sometimes our highest moral values are employed in a manner that leads to moral demise and toxic human communities. Rev. Dr. Johnson recognized that the dissonance between her moral passions about love and justice needed to be addressed because these clashing moral values were causing moral injury to others, and perhaps to herself. Through prayer and collaboration with trusted colleagues, she was able to reset her moral compass and release her spirit to reconnect with her actual feelings of love and respect for her congregation and its members. The courage to see herself clearly, to rearrange her internal moral orientations, and to engage the congregation from a more receptive attitudinal stance was liberating for herself and for the congregation.

Habits of Mind Exercise: The Hypnagogic Soul— Collaborative Conversation with Myself

In the strategic examples presented so far, I focused on the collaboration of persons who share their inner dialogues with one another, joining together around what is interesting, exciting, and challenging to them. That is, I focused on interpersonal dimensions of collaborative moral engagement in the context of various moral challenges. But, the fact that we each have "inner dialogues" in the first place indicates that we are always having collaboration conversations within ourselves. We are in all sorts of conversations within our hearts and minds. In this section, I want to introduce a method to assist the soul to apply its internal collaborative conversations to moral challenges facing the person. Learning this habit of mind will expand the soul's capacity for self-regulation and contextual creativity in the face of moral challenges.

I call this exercise "Hypnagogic Dilemma Management."[13] I have used it for years in teaching and counseling, and in workshops with clergy and other professionals. I invite the reader to read the steps carefully, and then supply their own situations. This exercise may be used privately or in groups. Pastors may introduce it as a resource for those to whom they are providing moral guidance.

Step 1: Setting the Stage

Our psyches often reach an impasse because of conflicting values requiring action, or because we must make a moral choice before we are ready or willing to act. We become stuck: facing choices between good and evil, between lesser evils, between conflicting goods, and other options that challenge or discomfit us. This exercise helps us to draw on the privacy of our bodily life in collaboration with our soul and brain to engage these dilemmas and to move forward. Practice makes perfect, so be patient and persistent as you discipline yourself to develop this habit of mind and make it your own. You may find it useful to record these instructions and let your own voice guide you through the process when addressing your moral dilemma.

Step 2: Centering

Find a quiet space where you will not be interrupted. Lightly close your eyes. Breathe slowly and comfortably in natural rhythms. Release tension in your body as you become aware that you are tense. Be at home with yourself. Release feelings of self-criticism, stress, and fear. Affirm yourself compassionately: connect with your sense of being alive and the power of life within you. Release agendas, goals, plans, expectations of yourself. Let whatever comes into focus just be there. Let it remain as it will, or move on as it will. Receive it as a friend and be with it; in so doing you are being with yourself.

Step 3: Visualizing the Dilemma

When you are ready, let the moral conflict or conflicts you are sensing come into place at the feeling level. What are the two "right things" that seem to be in conflict? Feel them. Embrace them. Name them. Experience each side of the conflict or challenge. [For example, you may be conflicted between preparing a professional presentation or spending the evening with your family.]

Step 4: Engaging All Sides

Let yourself feel directly one side of the conflict. In this example, let yourself feel what it would be like to prepare the presentation: how powerful that would be, how positive it would feel to do this, and how glad you would be to do a good job on it. Feel the good feelings you would have when you complete the presentation and your audience is appreciative. Feel this fully. Push away any distractions.

Now, when you are ready, let yourself feel directly the other side of the conflict. In this example, feel how good it would be to spend the evening with your family. Imagine your way into this as fully as you can. Follow the same feelings you just followed about working on your presentation: the pleasure of being with your family, the good feelings that will come to you from their appreciation. Live into these feelings as fully as you can; do not be distracted by other thoughts or competing obligations.

Next, let yourself feel your heart and mind move rapidly back and forth between the two sides of the conflict: feel the good feelings about the presentation and the good feelings about the evening with the family. Feel and be present to each of these good things as they come up and move back and forth. Let your psyche receive the back-and-forthness of the two imagined activities. Do not try to solve anything, decide anything, or think of any actions. Just let the impasse be present to your feelings and mind, moving back and forth. Be patient with yourself. Let your mind work on its own. There is no hurry here.

Step 5: Receive the Resolution

Your mind, in an uncanny fashion, will offer you a resolution after a reasonably short period of back-and-forthness. Watch how your spirit takes you to a new place—to a release from the paralyzing dilemma to a sense of a way forward that will feel good and right to you. You will be clear about how you should best proceed, and you will feel emotionally and spiritually capable of doing it. [In the example, you might realize that you can spend the evening with your family and get up early in the morning to prepare your presentation.]

Step 6: Act on Your Resolution

Do not second-guess it! Do not "yes...but"! Act on it, and continue to process hypnagogically the new conflicts or impasses that emerge (they will—all the time!). If you act on the resolution, you will find that your life works better and your values align with your world in more productive ways. I hope so, anyway.

Step 7: Conclusion

Standing back from this exercise, how did I find it useful for my personal self-enhancement? What was useful? What was lacking? How might I strengthen the dialectic between my internal dialogue and its resolution in our more public communal engagement of moral dilemmas? What more might I need from those conversations and other sources of knowledge to enhance the value of this exercise?

For Further Reading

Chait, Jonathan. "The Lessons of Colin Kaepernick: Patriotism Looks Very Different at the End of the Obama Era." *New York Magazine*, September 5–18, 2016. https://issuu.com/min-mag/docs/new_york_magazine_-_september_5__20

Haidt, Jonathan. "Can a Divided America Heal?" TED video, 20:17, posted November 2016, www.ted.com/talks/jonathan_haidt_can_a_divided_america _heal/transcript?language=en.

Harding, Rosemarie Freeney, and Rachel Elizabeth Harding. *Remnants: A Memoir of Spirit, Activism, and Mothering.* Durham, NC: Duke University Press, 2015.

Shaw, Tamsin. "The Psychologists Take Power." *New York Review of Books,* vol. LXIII, no. 3 (February 25, 2016): 38–41.

Tillich, Paul. *The Courage to Be.* New Haven, CT: Yale University Press, 1952.

CHAPTER 7

Moral Injuries and Wounded Souls

Throughout this book I connect and differentiate three moral challenges: moral dissonance, moral dilemmas, and moral injury. All of these bear on the unavoidable task of orienting our moral compasses and traversing the moral landscape. We have seen various ways that handling moral dissonance and moral dilemmas can enhance personal and social living and prevent moral injury. However, moral dissonance and moral dilemmas can contribute to moral injury, and souls wounded by moral trauma bear enormous dissonance and beget complex dilemmas. We turn now to the challenges arising when moral injury takes place.

Recognizing Moral Injury

The pastoral healer is a physician of fractured souls. We injure our souls by failing to follow our moral compass, or when our moral compass becomes misdirected because of the harm others do to us. Physicians of the soul name and frame the wounds of the soul and the diseases of the spirit in order to engage a vital healing collaboration. The pastoral caregiver is also a guide with respect to setting and resetting broken moral compasses. In addition to moral discernment, pastoral healers assist with strategies to travel in the right directions morally speaking.

How do pastoral caregivers and other assisting parties recognize moral injuries and soul wounds? And, once recognized, how are they received and engaged? In short, how might the process of discovering and naming the soul's wounds also become a process of healing and recovering? This chapter will describe moral injury and portray its causes and consequences. Chapter 8 in part III on Reckoning and Repair will propose collaborative strategies for moral healing and soul repair.

Moral injury refers to the diminishment of vitality that comes about in our souls and communities when we are unable to do what we believe is right or when doing the right thing results in harm to others and distress to ourselves. Moral injury can range from small moral "nicks, bruises, and broken bones" to a fatal injury, including death of the body and soul. Persons and communities might even commit moral suicide. Examples of fatal moral injury and moral suicide might be rape, child abuse, genocide, and committing crimes against humanity in war and political actions. I know of persons who have participated in each of these events who, by their own accounts if not in the eyes of others, are beyond the possibility of recovery. The cost to them was the permanent loss of their humanity; one soldier had tattooed on his leg: "My innocence for your freedom." Healing from a lost innocence is not innocence regained. It is innocence mourned and moral integrity reestablished. This is definitely possible, but not always realized.

We prevent moral injury by discerning and following our moral codes in the conflicting circumstances of everyday living. We heal from moral injury by reexamining our moral codes and revising our values and behaviors in light of new considerations. Moral injury is not necessarily the result of a traumatic event, such as killing in war or sexual and domestic violence. In fact, most often moral injury is seen in the small nicks, cuts, and bruises arising from micro-moral exchanges within ourselves and between others: unkind thoughts, failure to listen and understand, gossip, and stinginess, to name a few. We injure ourselves by the thousand minor cuts inflicted on ourselves and others, arising from knowing better but not doing better. In the complex social arenas of daily living, we make constant trade-offs between what we think is best and what we actually do. The gap that arises in this territory is a form of moral injury that over time can coagulate into hardening of our moral arteries, so to speak, and diminish vital and robust living.

The term moral injury has grown out of veteran spiritual care in the last few years. It attempts to offer soul-level language to repair wounded souls and negotiate re-entry to civilian culture. As indicated in chapter 2, moral injury does not equate with post-traumatic stress but can also be connected with it. Moral injury and post-traumatic stress and post-traumatic stress disorder sometimes need careful attention by both psychotherapeutic specialists and spiritual caregivers.[1]

I do not find it helpful to limit the concept of moral injury to singular traumatic events or to veteran spiritual care, though there is much to learn about the wide-ranging nature and dynamics of moral injury from care of veterans and from trauma-generated moral wounding. In my view, we do best with the concept of moral injury when we place it the context of everyday moral living. The concept of moral injury is best employed to explore the outcomes of a wide variety of moral engagements and to evaluate them in terms of the moral health or vitality of individuals and communities. It braids us into a common human enterprise of moral discernment, moral action, and moral recovery. In this respect we can become better companions, guides, and healers to one another on the moral journeys we are taking through the challenging moral landscapes within our own souls and among the moral energies clanging against themselves in our worlds of work, ministry, worship, war, politics, finance, and diverse cultural codes. By realizing how we are all in this together, and that moral living and moral injury exists across spectrums of mutual influence, we might find that the foundational spiritual principle that affirms "if we can share it, we can bear it," extends to the moral arenas of our living as well as to other challenging contingencies.

As social beings we need one another's assistance to face the moral challenges affecting our lives together and heal from the injuries we bring upon ourselves and one another in the moral cauldrons of living. Like it or not, we are conjoined in an enterprise of assisting one another to heal morally wounded souls and to reconstitute and strengthen the morally impaired human communities of which we are a part. Succinctly put, each of us is a morally injured and morally injuring individual, living in morally injured and morally injured communities, who need one another's assistance in moving beyond moral injury to moral health and vital living.

What Is the Soul?

Since we are focusing on moral injuries to the soul, it is important to remind the reader that the soul is an integrative process at the center of persons and communities. The soul is the integrating center of awareness, meaning, and value of the cumulative pain, joy, pleasure, and sensibilities of the human body and the body politic. It is the site of our deepest pain and our most sacred aspirations and values. Moral injury breaks apart its wholeness and stains its purity. Because the soul is also contextually creative, it is the site where healing and transformation may evolve. It is an enduring reality that is also changing for good and ill.

Moral Injury and Trauma

The soul of individuals and communities may be wounded by a variety of circumstances. Events in everyday living may diminish one's sense of worth and destabilize one's moral gyroscope. Common or acute moral dissonance can rise to the level of soul wounding. The outcomes of moral dilemmas may diminish the soul, leaving an enduring wound. And various forms of traumatic circumstances can result in moderate to severe damage to the soul's moral center. This section describes the relation between traumatic circumstances and soul wounds, often called moral trauma or moral injury.

Most broadly speaking, trauma is the disruption of our wholistic sense of life by unwanted, uncontrollable, and intrusive circumstances and events that damage our integrity and threaten our existence. More specifically, trauma is the unwanted life-altering disruption of one's bodily wholeness, personal dignity, and social network resulting from disaster, violence, precarious environments, poor judgments, and other less dramatic life-constricting or life-threatening situations. Trauma rips apart the fabric of life and raises unavoidable questions of life's meaning and goodness.

What are the sources of trauma-induced moral injuries? I have found it helpful to think of four intersecting conditions that give rise to various forms of trauma, including moral injury.

The most common condition giving rise to trauma is an *explosive assault*. Whether as witness, victim, or perpetrator, it is extremely traumatic to be in the presence of verbal or physical violence, especially when there is the threat or reality of death. Any such activity received, witnessed, or perpetrated raises acute moral questions. Why did this happen? What did I do to deserve this? Why did I lose my temper and behave so badly? Why did I not have enough courage to intervene or prevent the violence? What is the right response to what I did or to what happened to me: retaliation, self-punishment, lawsuit, forgiveness, restitution, or reconciliation?

There are traumatic explosive assaults from nature and history, as well as from interpersonal and social living. A tornado, earthquake, flood, hurricane, or other kind of natural disaster is a form of trauma rendered by explosive assault. War, terrorist acts, school shootings, and other explosive violence arising among conflicted social groups are fraught with traumatic consequences and moral interpretation. Sexual and domestic violence and public bullying of sexual minorities are examples of explosive assault leading to moral injury and requiring moral assessment. Are the people evil who did this? What are the morally acceptable options I have of protecting myself and holding them accountable? Are there ways in which I and my cohort are implicated? What is a good God's relation to this moral evil?

The second set of conditions giving rise to trauma is benign, constricted, and dangerous environments. I call these *pythonic habitats*. Pythons are stealthy snakes whose presence renders what might appear to be a beautiful or safe environment into something potentially deadly. A pythonic habitat is an environment that disrupts our well-being by squeezing the life out of us slowly, silently, against our will, or beyond our survival capacities. When gripped by these environments, we lose vitality, integrity, and the capacity for holistic living. Perpetual vigilance and low-grade threat squeeze our lives into small dollops of triviality. Examples are families with limited resources who have members deployed into combat environments, psycho-abusive marriages, poverty, illness, and other debilitating and potentially perilous situations.

Living on the brink of danger has a traumatic consequence, both in what it might lead to as well as the internally restricting outcomes.

To think of trauma as restricting rather than explosive might to some seem like a stretch. Does the concept of trauma cover everything that we do not like? Is any negative experience also a traumatic event or circumstance? Or are some things better left out of the category? Perhaps. But, in my study and work with veterans, I have learned that there is a growing awareness of the moral trauma that takes place by many who are in isolated war-making environments such as missile silos and drone warfare command centers. In the case of those with access to nuclear triggers, the benign safety from explosive assault is morally costly, whether or not they have to send a bomb or missile somewhere. And those who direct drone warfare report the stressful effects of the isolation, remoteness, and relative "benign normality" of their everyday lives. They frequently live at home with their families, go to work all day to wreak havoc on the nation's assumed enemies all over the globe, and return home to hang out and barbecue with the family. This benign, constrictive habitat is more dissonant and traumatic than we recognize. And it does not yet rise to the level of qualifying for the more established view of trauma as being a victim, perpetrator, or bystander to an explosive assault such as those faced more directly by combat personnel. Thus, it has proved difficult for veterans who served in these contexts to have their PTS symptoms recognized as war-related and treatment worthy.

A variant on trauma-inducing pythonic habitats might be seen in the pervasive number of trauma-informed environments.[2] For example, some public schools are trauma-informed contexts. Military sexual assault has created an unsafe environment for many women in the military. Communities recovering from various shootings (school, church, and theatres) are trauma-sensitive environments. These environments have two qualities. First, they are filled with individuals who have trauma histories and are living out of trauma narratives in relation to each other in their current social context. Such trauma histories contribute to a pythonic habitat that frequently explodes into various forms of verbal and physical assault.

Second, trauma-informed systems themselves become trauma generators because they do not often have the tools, structure, and resources to prevent and heal from the trauma brought to them by their post-traumatic members. Because of these trauma-related dynamics, schools may become sites of bullying, violence, and various forms of real or threatened physical and emotional harm. Military sexual assault is another example of a pythonic habitat that is infested with post-traumatic influences from which escape is impossible, even when accountability and punishment have occurred for past infractions. Trauma-informed local systems, therefore, may themselves become a source of trauma. When that happens, there is a loss of confidence that our communities can support our moral aspirations or fulfill our legal obligations to one another. This loss of confidence is a form of moral injury. It actually erodes the moral sense that our communities are strong enough to do the right thing in preventing harm and healing from past forms of trauma, including moral trauma.

A third source of trauma is *the road wrongly taken*. Moral injury occurs when people and groups make wrongheaded choices. Faced with dissonance and dilemma, the moral actor chooses a course of action that turns out to be traumatic for them and for others. Who among us has not wished we had done otherwise? We wish we had stood up for our values rather than caved in. We wish we had chosen the other course now that hindsight has revealed the disastrous consequences of what we did (and, therefore, what we did not do). Sometimes our behavioral and moral choices do not result from anything as focused as a specific moral dilemma. Sometimes they result from unwittingly choosing circumstances that lead to traumatic demise over time by failing to recognize the dangers beforehand, or to tend properly to the consequences that come into place after we have embarked on a course of action.

A fourth form of trauma leading to or arising from moral injury is *grievous loss*. I gained this insight most clearly from my colleague, Nancy Ramsay. Through her work with the Soul Repair think tank at Brite Divinity School, Ramsay recognized that loss of one's moral compass through participation in war is not only a symptom of moral injury, but a source.[3] Another good example of how grievous loss can be a source of moral injury is disclosed in the moral challenges of the Burkett family, reported above in the strategic example on "God: My Moral Enemy." The demise of cherished parents and a vulnerable child led Mr. Burkett to lose his moral center and source of spiritual renewal. Loss, in the case of moral injury, therefore can have two dimensions. First, there is the loss of something significant in a person's life and identity, and, second, a loss of an intact moral compass because of how one interprets life's catastrophes.

What, then, is moral injury? Trauma becomes moral injury when the actors and recipients find their moral centers to be disrupted by what others did to them or by what they did to others in the traumatic events in which they were victims, witnesses, or perpetrators. The most common forms of moral injury are the personal diminishment and moral challenges that result when individuals and communities recognize that they failed to live in accordance with their moral values. In these cases, moral injury refers to the impairment that results because we acted against our moral center and feel regret for what happened. When responded to positively, moral injury sets us into a new obligatory relationship with ourselves and with those we harmed.

Features of Wounded Souls

What is it like to bear soul wounds? To identify symptoms of moral injury is like mapping a vast ocean. Navigating the ocean takes good maps and compasses—and a lot of trial and error. We are in deep waters. There are many captains insisting that their routes are best. What follows is a guide for understanding and engaging various levels of moral injury. It can be used by the specialist, or for self-reflection by a morally wounded person. It is a useful basis for conversation with friends, colleagues, students, parishioners, and others we serve. It can be used for self-assessment and community support in social groups such as families, schools, and congregations. It is a promising adjunct to spiritual direction. And it can be a foundation for more technical psychotherapeutic practice. I try to use language that portrays the sensibilities of the soul of the morally injured, whether these are available to consciousness at a given time or not. As the reader will see, these categories marking soul wounds are generated, maintained, made available, and mitigated through the dynamic interplay of the human soul embodied in culture, time, and history. They are suitable for everyday moral injuries as well as the unique life-changing cataclysms of war, natural disaster, and other major life disruptions.

What sense of the self, world, and God remains for the person and group suffering from the soul wound coming from moral injuries?[4] Four anchor points need to be mentioned at this stage. First, it is most helpful to consider that post-traumatic difficulties are not contained events and partialized elements of a person's life. They are pervasive, ongoing, and permanent substructures of the soul. Trauma creates a pervasive new consciousness that becomes part of the architecture of the psyche, whether known or unknown. I do not make a hard and fast distinction between trauma in general and moral trauma specifically. I believe that they are separable, but interdependent. Trauma sets up a post-traumatic consciousness comprised of many elements, including moral dimensions. I will focus on the ongoing moral dimensions, but not separate them too firmly from other forms of trauma. Neither do I think of trauma and the fairly permanent morally traumatic-informed consciousness as a one-off past event. It is an ongoing substructure of one's being, which has different expressions and valences in specific contexts over time.

The second anchor point in this discussion, as will be shown in the following list of the six characteristics of a trauma-informed consciousness, are best seen as interrelated rather than separate and linear. It helps to lay them out in a list form in order to gain a conceptual grasp and to guide conversation. But they are not a diagnostic checklist. They are not evenly distributed in any given person or social group. Finding their valence in pastoral care is part of the art of ministry that is made possible by collaborative exploration and openness to discovery in concrete caregiving relationships.

The third anchor point is the recognition that these elements of a morally injured consciousness are fully applicable to many aspects of community trauma and moral injury, as well as to individual psyches. Further, the trauma may have been experienced most directly by one or more individuals and communities, but because

"I am as we are" any moral challenge, injury, or advance causes a ripple effect through the system lasting for generations, whether known or not.

The fourth anchor point is the realization that the fairly clear conceptual categories I offer are not necessarily matched by rational processes in persons suffering from moral injury. Naming a category may make the helper more comfortable but it may have little positive effect on how the person in pain experiences their reality. In fact, it may lead to angry feelings and broken relationships because of the dissonance between rational discourse and irrational energies. Those bearing markers of moral injury may function at a precognitive level and be put off by such labels and categories. Trauma often removes the conditions for naming our experience. Brain processes can overtake ego control and behavioral self-regulation. Toning down the brain and finding ways to self-regulate dangerous and out-of-control emotional and behavioral reactions are often preliminary but necessary steps to regaining health and agency. Healing is more than labeling and conveying diagnostic nomenclature. It involves costly and disciplined immersion into dangerous and elusive territory. It requires all the presence, compassion, wisdom, patience, and strength everyone can muster.

In spite of these cautions, having usable conceptual handholds can give us a place to grasp as we seek to climb out of the morass. By naming our wounds we are better able to join our brain and adaptive capacities to our lived realities. They are tools of resiliency and the foundation for contextual creativity. In addition to giving us something to hold on to, they give us a place to stand and understand. They give us someone to understand us and to stand with us. Conceptual categories that articulate our painful wounds may become stepping stones to repair and renewal. In the very least, they provide a means to explore collaboratively what remains for good and ill in the wounded soul.

We turn now to the characteristics of morally injured souls mentioned in the second anchor point above. Through them we see the directions we journey together toward healing, sustaining, and guiding in the pastoral care of morally injured persons and communities. Many of the examples are from the military context. They are selected because they sharply illustrate the consequences of moral injury for all who bear the burden of a wounded soul. It is also important to note that trauma is both a life event and a condition of the soul.

First, a soul injured by moral trauma exists in *time out of place*. Through flashbacks, ruminations, and memory, the past is not past. The past is pulled forward into the present. The past takes over our attention to the here and now. Moral trauma takes our consciousness backward to the pain that happened to us, and to shame and guilt for what we did. And because the pain is so great and the pull of the past is so strong, the capacity to imagine a positive future is diminished or even absent. Time becomes dislocated, oscillating, and not under our conscious control without healing and effort.

One of the greatest costs of trauma and moral injury is that it marks our conscious life from the time of its onset forward. It cuts off the significance of our lives and their richness before the event. In one sense, time before the trauma ceases to exist. Life begins with the trauma and defines our present, past, and future from that moment in time. Regaining this rich past is part of the reframing of trauma in order to engage it. Can the pre-traumatic past be regained as a source of resiliency and healing and restoring time into its proper alignment?

Second, a soul injured by moral trauma is animated by *a questing body*. Trauma always involves the body, both in terms of its effect on bodily health and on subsequent body-based emotional processes. A deployed soldier phoned his wife from the combat zone. He opened the conversation with these words: "I just killed my first man. Will you still touch me?" The moral injury from his traumatic experience was thoroughly bodily-mediated processes. His body was trained to kill. He successfully accomplished this task. He left a dead body somewhere in the world. But now his own body feels tainted. He is tremulously anxious that his wife will not want to touch him. He seeks a body that will be worthy of touch by his cherished life-companion. He fears that her moral revulsion might match his own and lead her to withdraw her body from his. He reaches desperately across the world on his cell phone for solace, reassurance, and human connection. It is a moment of incredible intimacy and abject terror for him.

The trauma she experiences is great as well. It binds them together in a quest for spiritual and bodily intimacy. She asks her pastor, "How can I let him know that I love him and that I want to touch him? Will he let me? Is he so full of remorse that he can't receive my love and touch? I want to touch him, but he is in another country across the world. What will all this mean for our relationship?" Indeed, will the husband's moral injury traumatize and morally wound their relationship? His moral injury has set up a potentially dangerous dissonance between them. If that dissonance rises to the level of a moral dilemma between touching and not touching, or being emotionally isolated or emotionally connected, there are potentially great negative consequences at hand.

The literature is replete with examples of the loss of bodily integrity that results from trauma and moral injury. Sometimes there is physical impairment, loss of limbs, and a variety of other injuries to the brain, organs, and various bodily systems. The quest for healing is the quest for an intact and restored body.

Sometimes the quest to still the spiritual and physical pain leads to self-medication, drug and alcohol addiction, compulsive sexual activity, and placing the body in harm's way through reckless behaviors. Sometimes the capacity for intimate sexual pleasure and relational intimacy is lost altogether. Some of the actions they take in search of restored bodily wholeness, deepen bodily alienation and the gap between bodies and souls. Fighting, violence, and compulsive physical feats are modes of bodily experience indicating that body and soul are disconnected and that the body is on a trauma-driven quest for punishment and/or healing.

A third expression of a soul injured by moral trauma is a pattern of *ambivalent loyalties*. In my work with veterans and their families, I have learned that many face a normal challenge of negotiating the bi-loyal relational commitments that come from close bonds with battle mates. The primary bond for most military personnel when they are deployed for combat is with their friends, family, and the communities they are leaving. During their deployments, they inevitably become bonded to their comrades and primarily obligated to them, the mission, and their command structure. A new set of bonded loyalties and moral codes comes into place. The bonded loyalties and moral codes in the combat environment become dominant; the loyalties at home are vital but not central in the day-to-day social structure of deployed military units. The codes of the warrior and the codes of the civilian exist side by side within a body and soul devoted to each. The bi-loyal commitment to the service member's comrades and civilian life becomes a permanent feature of the service person's identity. In the best of all possible worlds, this bi-loyalty is a positive and mutually reinforcing configuration. In terms of moral injury, when these loyalties become dissonant because the codes of one conflict with the codes of the other, moral dilemmas and relational challenges may become dangerous and damaging.

Normal bi-loyal commitments are not in themselves morally dissonant or morally injurious. But when they come into conflict and a person acts against one side of their internalized loyalties, moral injury is the result. At that point, normal bi-loyal commitments may become sources of profound conflict and self-condemnation. Individuals and communities become trapped in the dissonance between core loyalties and ambivalent about the relationship to each. Rather than becoming a source of enrichment and creativity, they diminish vital living.

Other forms of ambivalent relationships indicate moral injury. For example, a person who has failed their moral code may not feel worthy or capable of sustaining their commitments to another person, job, faith, community, or even to themselves. They live in the pull and push of closeness and distance, commitment and rejection. In a word, they are ambivalently attached. Ambivalent attachments may result from moral injury perpetrated by the actor. They may also result from being traumatized by others. When people violate our trust and break relational commitments, without healing we too can become ambivalently attached to ourselves and our worlds. We may not be able to make reliable relational commitments. We may isolate and distance ourselves without apparent cause or warning. Or we might become enmeshed and overly fused with someone or some endeavor that stifles relational and personal creativity. In these circumstances, persons are insecurely attached, ambivalent about their loyalties, and suffering from the lack of a nurturing reciprocal connection to their world. Understanding these predictable features of trauma and moral injury can relieve the sufferer. Finding safe ways to explore the tensions within bi-loyal commitments and ambivalent attachments is a crucial first step toward recovering the capacity for learning to trust again and living well, relationally speaking. The hypnagogic process of engaging dissonant elements in one's soul can be a resource for blending ambivalent loyalties.

Fourth, a soul injured by moral trauma is gripped by *moral ambiguities*. There are two central moral concerns we have as humans: "Am I doing the right thing?" and "Am I a good person?" These questions never go away, though they may not always be consciously motivating questions. In a morally saturated world, however, there is no escaping the pervasive moral obligations that require our response. And there is no escaping that we will evaluate ourselves and be evaluated by others about how well we engaged them. It is in our nature to want to be good and to do right.

The morally injured person struggles to know whether they did the right thing and whether they are good persons, even if they failed to do the right thing. The answer to this question is sometimes straightforward and clear. "I did do the right thing." "I feel good about who I am." "I did the best I could with what I had in those circumstances." Moral compromise and moral choices most often line up in the "doing right and being good" column of our moral calculations.

But sometimes the answer to the question of goodness is unclear or negative. "I don't think I did the right thing or that I am fundamentally a good person." "I screwed up!" "I made bad choices. I was selfish. I was violent. I hurt a lot of people. Someone had to stop me." There is no ambiguity when a person or group is able to recognize and take responsibility for their moral failures. Having the moral courage to take responsibility for one's behaviors and values and to change one's identity and moral codes is a sign of health and strength.

The morally injured and injuring party, however, lives in a more ambivalent moral culture, both internally and publicly. A combat veteran takes actions in combat that sometimes come into question in civilian life. The context of battle and the context of civilian life sometimes operate on different moral codes. What makes a warfighter virtuous in war sometimes makes that person a monster in civilian life. Or a military chaplain whose moral code is pacifistic may feel compromised by serving soldiers and the military that exists to be a lethal force to protect others from harm. The moral ambiguity that arises in these conditions can be debilitating, leading to a chronic moral disease of self-doubt and moral stasis. It can result in a profound alienation from a sense of life's goodness and one's own virtue.

Part of the moral aftermath of war is the ambiguous set of feelings and unclear responsibilities of who is responsible for what and how we should act now. Do those living now have moral obligations from offenses in the past? Pauline Boss has a category of grieving that she calls "ambiguous loss."[5] Ambiguous loss occurs when it is impossible to complete a grieving process because the information needed about what happened to the body and the circumstances of death are permanently unavailable. How does one let go of someone who is not gone? Ramsay suggests that ambiguous loss also occurs uniquely for morally injured veterans who are present in their bodies, but whose soul and spirit were lost when they lost their moral compasses in war.[6] Accordingly, the moral aftermath of trauma and moral injury includes questions about how to properly assess responsibility. And, once assessed, how to act to undertake meaningful restitution, change, and reconciliation. When the avenues of resolution are closed, the morally injured parties are stuck in the limbo of ambiguity. The restlessness, cynicism, guilt, and futility arising from moral ambiguity are potentially fatal diseases of the wounded soul.

Our personal moral ambiguity links directly to the macrosystemic level. The human community has come to the moral awareness of a trans-historical responsibility for the cruelties of the past. On the macrosystemic level, nations and social groups are coming to accept that they are morally implicated in the harm they do to others in time and history. But how this is accomplished and how citizens buy into it are difficult matters. There is considerable moral ambiguity about trans-historical responsibility for moral injuries of the past. Though many accept the benefits of what was made possible by the "sins of our fathers," there is less commitment on the part of the beneficiaries to repair the wounds and restore the resources that were taken from others for their benefit. Meanwhile, those who suffer from these historical injustices continue to bear the moral wounds and trauma that have been engendered. The moral ambiguity arising from our communal history persists. The claims of history become a source of moral conflict as well as the remnants of a diseased moral culture. In any case, recovering from moral injury may not be possible without some capacity to move through moral ambiguity to moral accountability from which justice, forgiveness, reconciliation, and repair might come about.[7]

Fifth, a soul injured by moral trauma is hampered by *defective agency*. To be a moral actor and to heal from moral injury requires personal agency. Personal agency is the capacity to self-regulate, to act with integrity from one's moral centers, and to take responsibility for one's actions and their consequences. Personal agency also involves setting limits on the actions of others, protecting oneself from harm, and employing healing strategies when injured and injuring. Personal agency is the energy that makes contextual creativity possible.

Moral injury results from (and leads to) defective moral agency. When I am not able to act on my core values, it is often because I have an impaired or defective agential capacity. And when I am injured by the moral impairments or moral choices of others, my capacity to be myself and act from a vital core is diminished, if not destroyed. Moral injury, whether because of my own actions or the actions of others, skews my personal power and renders it harmful or ineffective. I have lost the ability to realize my intentions. My capacity to cope and recover escapes my will. I lose my agency by becoming isolated and cut-off, or enmeshed and controlled by others. I lose the capacity to self-soothe. Self-care becomes difficult. Self-compassion is replaced with self-disgust. When coupled with moral ambiguity, the morally injured party is unable to make plausible moral assessments and act effectively to resolve intractable moral conflicts. They become disoriented about what is the right thing for them to do or unable to properly act on what appears to be the best direction to take.

I discovered a complicated dynamic between defective agency and theological views of God in an incest survivor's recovery group. A family therapist friend invited me to join the group as a theological consultant to discuss issues of power and agency. She wanted me to share a theological view of God's power that she had heard in one of my workshops. She thought that her group of Christian women might find it useful in their healing from being violated by fathers and other family members.

In my meeting with the recovery group, I learned that many of the women felt shame that they did not have the power to stop their violation. They felt shame that they did not have power to heal from the injury. And they felt ambivalent about how to hold the abuser accountable when at some level they felt that what happened was their fault. In addition, they articulated a deep sense that God might have intended this to happen to them for some higher good or to punish them for some moral failing. After all, God is omnipotent and good, so if God did not want this to happen he would have used his power to stop it. In their minds, God's agency is always perfect and never defective. Therefore, to use their personal power against their violator and against God's will seemed wrong to them. They were stuck, even though in other ways considerable healing and empowerment had taken place.

The gist of my perspective was something like this:

The core issue here is how we think of personal and divine agency, or power. Some interpretations of divine power think that since God is omnipotent whatever happens is ultimately for a higher purpose or to account for past wrongs. The thought here is that human power is only legitimate power when it joins or reflects God's power. It is not creative or free in its own right. When exercised freely, it is dangerous, selfish, and wrong; it leads to harm of self and others. This is the dominant or default view of divine and human power.

I then articulated another view:

There are Christian theological teachings about power that say that to be real, to have life, is to have some measure of power and agency. Without power and agency there is no vital life and no capacity for love, intimacy, creativity, and morally responsible living. Because every living entity has some power, God's power is not omnipotent in the sense that it can, even if it wanted to, control all actions and outcomes. While God has the greatest degree of power possible, and that power is always linked to divine goodness (it is never an agent of evil), God does not have all the power it is to possible to have in the universe. That means there is finite freedom and unique agency for every entity in the vastness of the cosmos. Your abuser did not act as an agent of divine power or intention; they acted on their own power against God's intentions. Their agency violated your agency; at that time in your life you did not have the power to prevent their abusive use of their power. God is on your side in protesting this abuse and empowering you to heal from it. Likewise, God always lends divine power to your efforts, but your efforts or power must also be forthrightly available. Power is a conjoined reality, not a dispensed one.

A rich and complex conversation followed my pedantic overture. One of the women said that she never felt free to confront her father or to refuse to attend events where he was present because she thought that doing so would be against God's will and that she would not be able to stand up to her father when she saw him. It was difficult for her to shift the locus of power to her own agency. The group helped her see how she might claim her agency to address her ambivalence about attending her beloved brother's wedding when her hated father would also be there. When she shifted the locus of power to herself, the group helped her decide not to attend the wedding but to carve out a special time with her brother and his new wife to celebrate their marriage. She felt relieved at this decision. There was a twinge of guilt about "acting selfishly and maybe displeasing God." But she understood that these feelings came from another setting on her moral compass (so to speak). In spite of these ambivalent feelings, she knew that this new direction was best for her.

Another woman reported that hearing our conversation made her realize that she had been too down on herself for letting herself be picked up in a bar and having sex with a stranger over the weekend. She had shared this event and her self-disgust earlier in the session. She indicated that her struggle with sexual promiscuity had been a pattern of living since her abuse by an uncle. She hated herself because she did not have the personal strength to stop it. On deeper inspection, she said, "I think I didn't believe I was worthy of stopping bad things since I hadn't stopped my uncle. Maybe I was not thinking right. If what you say about power is true, then I have more than I think and I can get better about using it. I also realize that I keep waiting for God to rescue me. That may be unrealistic."

Defective moral agency is a hallmark of moral injury. Its opposite is moral courage and moral efficacy. Both moral courage and moral efficacy are always possible to learn and implement because each entity, whether personal, social, cultural, natural, or historical, has a significant potential for moral agency and contextual creativity. To have life is to have power, even if at times the power is meager. In the sections following, other examples will be provided of how to name and frame various forms of moral injury so that they may be engaged in a healing and contextually creative manner.

Sixth, a soul injured by moral trauma is *spatially averse*. The world is a dangerous place for traumatized and morally injured persons. The associations of place and injury are carried in the brain and can be activated at any time. Hence, many perpetrators and victims of moral injuries, or those living in explosive, toxic, and pythonic moral habitats, are often hypervigilant and do everything they can to protect themselves. Objects in time and space can take on a threatening complexion, whether or not they are harmful. For example, one veteran I know said that for the first year back after a combat deployment he could hardly drive his car under bridges and highway overpasses because of the terror that a sniper or terrorist group was positioned to attack. Similarly, a female survivor of sexual abuse by her minister said that she could not kneel at the altar rail to receive communion. She had to stand and receive the elements in her hands, preferably by a female minister, because the associations of the abuse were too overwhelming when kneeling at the altar rail. The holy sacrament became a symbol of bodily and spiritual violation rather than a means of strength, healing, and new life. Fortunately, she was able to structure her body in space in such a manner that the sacrament was a spiritual gift for her. But it took some spiritual counsel and regaining her personal agency for this to become the case.

Moral injury and trauma take place in history. They occur in time and space. As we have seen, they dislocate our sense of time, and they infuse the places we go with threat and terror. The very existence of our bodies in time and space render them vulnerable, as well as agents of beauty, creativity, and pleasure. Post-traumatic moral injury heightens the natural anxiety about living in the world. It brings past injuries into present consciousness, restricting our options and diminishing our well-being.

Ta-Nehisi Coates writes about the traumatic and traumatizing social spaces in which black bodies live. His focus is on black male bodies. In his prize-winning book *Between the World and Me*, Coates identifies two threats to the black male body: the culture of violence that has grown up in black communities, and the centuries-old violations through slavery, lynching, and police shootings by a white, privileged, racist society.[8] For Coates, it is the black body that exists between the violent world and his particular soul and identity. The trauma and violence against the black body means that everyday living in all times and places is dangerous. There is danger wherever black bodies are seen, wherever they go. Vigilance is perpetually required. Coates helps us to see that spatial aversion is built into the consciousness of black men. The morally toxic racist society has ongoing debilitating consequences for the life-chances and vitality of black people in general and black males in particular. In my view, healing from racist moral injury involves two major changes. First, the racist society that engenders harm against blacks must reorient its moral compass toward "liberty and justice for all." Black lives must matter. Black must be beautiful everywhere. Second, those struggling to resist and heal from the harm done to them must be clear about the moral compasses they use to orient themselves to one another and to resist and work toward transforming the social structures that are so harmful to their bodies and souls.

To summarize and conclude, moral injury is a complex condition that arises from a variety of explosive events, constrictive and dangerous environments, poor choices, and grievous losses. It may also arise from the intractability of everyday moral dissonance and the outcome of moral dilemmas. Morally injured souls may take actions that intensify preexisting soul wounds. Moral injury may indicate a moral failure on the part of an acting individual or the practices and actions of social groups. Moral injury can also be the consequences for victims of the actions of morally injured actors. In either case, moral injury has ongoing consequences for bodies and souls. The dislocated consciousness and spiritual frame that arises from the aftermath of moral injury have six interrelated features. There is a pervasive temporal dislocation in which past, present, and future senses of time are blurred, confused, and debilitating. Morally injured persons are questing for healed bodies, the restoration of bodily integrity, and the reunification of body and soul. Morally injured persons struggle with ambivalent loyalties between moral codes, peer group cohorts, and relational attachments. They are faced with challenging moral ambiguities about motivations for their actions, lines of responsibility, and proper accountability. Morally injured persons are victims diminished by defective agency, both by others who harmed them and their own responses after the injury. And morally injured persons struggle to find safe spaces for their bodies and souls. They are perpetually averse to spaces and places where injury is likely or feared to occur. Strategies for naming, framing, enacting, and revising moral realities in the face of moral injury will be developed in the Reckoning and Repair section.

Habits of Mind Exercise

Take a few minutes to write some notes on your inner dialogue as you read though these ideas and examples of trauma-induced moral injury. What was interesting to you? What was exciting? What seemed usable? What was challenging? Where did you fight with the text? What questions does it raise? Take a few more minutes to think of a moral injury in your life, or in your community's. Briefly write it down. Then make six columns with the six elements of a morally injured consciousness heading each. Fill in how your soul wounds link to those categories. If new categories suggest themselves to you as you do this exercise, add them to the mix (or modify the existing categories as needed). List the things you are doing to address them. Identify what still needs to be healed or worked through. Imagine some strategies you can take to engage your challenges. Save these notes for the section on Reckoning and Repair and see if you find further assistance there.

For Further Reading

Brock, Rita Nakashima, and Gabriella Lettini. *Soul Repair: Recovering from Moral Injury after War*. Boston: Beacon, 2012.

Junger, Sebastian. *Tribe: On Homecoming and Belonging*. New York: Twelve, 2016.

McDonald, Joseph, ed. *Exploring Moral Injury in Sacred Texts*. Philadelphia: Jessica Knightly Publishers, 2017.

Sherman, Nancy. *The Untold War: Inside the Hearts, Minds, and Souls of Our Soldiers*. New York: Norton, 2010.

White, Michael, and D. Epston. *Narrative Means to Therapeutic Ends*. New York: Norton, 1991.

Part III

Reckoning and Repair

CHAPTER 8

Healing the Wounded Soul

Reviewing Moral Injury

Moral injury refers to the diminishment of vitality that comes about in our souls and communities when we are unable to do what we believe is right, or when wrongs are done to us. It also takes place when our doing the right thing results in harm to others and distress to ourselves, in spite of our intentions.

We prevent moral injury by discerning and following our moral codes in the conflicting circumstances of everyday living. We heal from moral injury by taking account of the moral injuries that we cause and bear. Healing includes reexamining our moral codes and revising our values and behaviors in the light of the consequences to ourselves and others our actions have brought about.

Now that we are turning explicitly to the healing of souls wounded by moral injury, what happened to our earlier concern about the body? Is it now time to leave the body behind and fasten our stethoscopes exclusively to the soul? After all, this book is about "repairing wounded souls." As we turn to healing the soul, it is important to remind ourselves about the relationship between the body and the soul.

As we have seen earlier, bodies and souls are co-terminus, co-generative, and perpetually interconnected. Though interconnected, the body and the soul are not one and the same. They stand in a collaborative dynamic relationship to one another. We can begin with the soul and learn very quickly how the body is faring, where it hurts and where it is vital. Messages from the soul can give persons strength and perspective when bodies fail. The body is also a window into how the soul is faring—where it feels alive and hopeful and where it is dissipated or demoralized. The soul can be enlivened through massage, exercise, diet, and other caring ministrations. Collaboration between bodies and souls enhances the capacity to hold on, heal, and sustain vital living even when circumstances are difficult.

In this chapter, I will profile what is meant by healing bodies and souls from moral injury. What can we expect to result from engaging the moral wounds born in our souls and bodies? What kind of helping partnership will lead to healing and restoration of vital living? In the following chapter, I will profile specific strategies and interactions by which to create healing collaborative conversations.

The Nature of Healing

Healing is a complicated term. Its meaning can range from "restoration of prior wholeness" to "empowerment for greatest possible function." A person who broke a leg can expect to be restored to prior wholeness when the leg is set. However, a person who lost a leg would experience healing differently than getting back their original leg. They would experience healing as a cessation of pain and successful adaptation to a prosthetic leg. Such a person might well regard themselves as fully healed and fully whole, in spite of the absence of their original leg. In this case, healing is best considered as "restoration of functional wholeness," rather than as "restoration of prior wholeness."[1]

Healing in both of these examples includes finding a way through the grief that resulted from their injuries, and the various psychological, relational, vocational, and spiritual losses that may have resulted. When we are injured physically, spiritually, relationally, and morally, there is a sense of loss. It may come in the form of self-disgust for carelessness or for possessing some flaw in ourselves. The sense of loss attending moral injury may involve anger at life or at God. It may engender sadness, depression, isolation, and even despair. Asking, "What have you lost from this injury? What will not happen in your life now that this has taken place?" may help the injured to begin to name the grief in order to frame grieving as a healing resource. In any case, healing from the losses attending moral injury includes constructive grieving of those losses. So, to begin, healing can be a process of restoring prior wholeness or of achieving the highest possible level of functional wholeness once the grief and loss resulting from the injury are engaged realistically and positively.

But there is more. The heart of healing moral injury involves discerning proper accountability for the injury and taking realistic action to make up for the harm one caused and received. As we have seen, moral ambiguity and defective agency are defining symptoms of moral injury. Gaining moral health includes gaining an empowering sense of what each party is and is not responsible for. Taking unnecessary moral burdens off the injured party makes it more possible for them to bear their own burdens and to find a contextually creative agency to revisit the harm they carry from a position of strength.

In addition, moral healing restores effective personal agency expressed as the ability to live in the present, with a nonreactive relationship to the past or a fearfully anxious orientation to the future. The capacity to self-regulate from a self-affirming rather than self-judging stance is a mark of healing symptoms of time out of place and of overcoming aversion to entering certain physical and social environments. Healing moral injury restores as much as possible the agency necessary to live comfortably in time and space, and to regulate the infusion of strain into one's consciousness from past memories and reactions.

A leading indicator of healing from moral injury is the ability once again to feel at home in the strength, vitality, and pleasure of one's body, including acceptance of its limitations. The body and the soul mirror one another. They draw strength from their interactions. When the life of the body is able to mediate positive forces, the other elements of healing become more apparent. Time is in place. Effective agency is present. Spaces and places can be negotiated with realistic caution. Loyalties become multilayered rather than ambivalent. Whatever shame, blame, and guilt remain becomes the basis for moving to whatever levels of forgiveness, restitution, and reconciliation are possible in the circumstances.

Now, a caveat. Early in the book, I indicated the metaphor "moral injury" is a leaky metaphor. I want to underscore here that the metaphor of "moral healing" is even leakier. It has a potential of causing greater harm by pressuring the injured to find their way to a state of being in which the injury is over and done with. One of the most harmful cultural mindsets is the expectation that traumatized people "will get over it and move on." We mistakenly turn health and healing into moral virtues, and create our heroes from those who endure, recover, and become the role models for everyone else. Worse, we think of healing as moving beyond brokenness, rather than blending into a dynamic whole the brokenness and resiliency that enables us simultaneously to bear the pain of our moral injuries and live vitally with what remains available to us.

The truth about moral injury is that, like all traumatic injury, it lingers and pervades. We carry it through life and across the generations. This is simply a fact. But, when healing is understood as "restoration to the greatest functional wholeness possible," the question is not whether healing the injury is completed, but how it is carried in the fuller tapestry of our lives. The coloration of the tapestry will always be infused by the coloration of our injuries. But that coloration blended with other colors in the fabric of our lives may not be blood-red. Or the blood-red segments of the design may be rather circumscribed in relation to the whole cloth. And the blood red of traumatic injury, when combined with other colors and patterns, may actually take on a complex beauty and interest. But the tapestry will always incorporate the coloration of trauma and the effects of moral injury will contribute to ongoing vulnerabilities and well as discovered vitalities and wisdom.

Mending Our Ways

The central feature of healing moral injury involves correction. We correct our moral courses by resetting our moral compasses, or by getting back on the proper bearings. We correct our mistakes and repair the damage they cause. However, "correction" is not a term that fits easily into the metaphor of "healing" because of its moralistic and judgmental connotations. But unless we take proper accountability for our part in our moral situation, it is impossible to find proper agency and to fashion contextually creative healing responses to our moral failures and wounded souls. We remain stuck in self-excuse, self-blame, or outrage toward others.

I find "mending our ways" to be an energizing metaphor in moral healing. It blends the medical and the moral in a safe, nonjudgmental manner. To mend something is to heal or repair it. We mend broken bones, wounded souls, and fractured relationships. Mending restores to either an original or a functional wholeness. But to mend is also to correct something that has become flawed or distorted or harmful. Mending recognizes the flaws that need correcting. The idea of mending emphasizes the positive result rather than the diminished or problematic starting point. It points toward the end-game rather than to the originating cause. In terms of moral healing, the call to "mend one's ways" is a call to take realistic responsibility for one's harmful actions and to address the harm done to us by others without blaming ourselves as victims.[2] It is a message of invitation and hope rather than of blame and condemnation. It blends medical and moral frames of reference in a creative synthesis of new possibilities.

The Caregiver's Standpoint

How does the pastoral caregiver go about providing moral guidance and healing? In the beginning of this book, I suggested that the pastoral guide had two core resources for working with moral concerns. The first resource is sharing the risks facing the careseeker. The second is joining the careseeker in co-creative discovery of the way through the moral terrain. The link between these is attunement and mutual active listening. The pastoral and spiritual caregiver knows that the direction of change, healing, and moral advances arise from the insights generated by the authentic relationship between the care provider and the careseeker as both engage in a safe partnership to address the difficult challenges before them. From this anxious, committed, collaborative attunement arises the possibility of contextually creative healing and moral betterment.

The key to this process of building a healing relationship is learning to listen from a particular standpoint. Listening in pastoral care involves listening with an invested interest in the experience and uniqueness of the other. We listen to learn. We listen to build collaborative relational bonds so that we might accomplish important things together. Both the listener and speaker have emotional and spiritual "skin in the game" with one another. If it is true that "I am as we are," then the difference between the caregiver and the careseeker is relatively differentiated by roles and context, but not by our humanity and our capacity for "mutual speaking and listening." Palaver is the core.[3]

It has been helpful for me to think of the relational partnership and exploratory inquiry built through pastoral listening as comprising a rather fulsome unit of experience and engagement. I playfully teach this point to my students this way: "As a pastoral caregiver, we cannot help others unless we prehend the total gestalt." Their response is almost always as I intend it to be: "Huh?"

So, what do I mean by "prehending the total gestalt?" Prehension is a term in process philosophy that points to our life in the universe, including our lives with ourselves and others, as the coming together of felt connections, usually below awareness. Life is felt; it comes to us non-verbally as well as verbally; it vibrates and hums as well as explodes. Our prehensions amalgamate into centers of experience, some of which are conscious. But whether conscious or not, our reality is at the felt level of our life in the world and we carry all matter of experience in our beings, mediated to our minds and souls through our bodies. It is the basis for "mutual speaking and listening," and for claiming that "I am as we are." And all that experience, whether known or not, has an influence on what is happening in the here and now, on how the past will be appropriated, and what kind of future will be possible. So, to help others we must be participatorily located within their total prehensive gestalt and its unique data set.

To prehend the total gestalt includes attention to our own process and the relational dynamic being created between us. Thus, when I say that pastoral care in moral injury means that we have to listen, I mean that we have to do more than listen to parts. To listen for the total gestalt means that we try to gain a comprehensive sensibility of the careseeker, and what they hope for from us to assist them with their concerns. To accomplish this, we listen to ourselves as well. We listen with our whole beings: imagination, thoughts, feelings, bodily sensations, influence of the room or setting, and our mental self-talk or inner dialogue. We listen through our personal and cultural histories as well. We need to be present to all of this in ourselves and others, since these elements are part of the total gestalt and contribute to what may come next. It is a mutual process of speaking and listening, perceiving and imagining, and joining or attuning to the other while maintaining one's own fluid center of experience.[4]

In the actual collaborative encounter about moral injury (or any other topic, for that matter), the "total gestalt" is a complex constellation of many parts and subparts of experience. But it is not an overwhelmingly massive totality as far as conscious awareness is concerned. It comes to precise focus in dissonance, dilemmas, and constricting impasses. The total gestalt is large, but it also has a focus. The focus of the gestalt identifies the concerns driving the person and requires immediate concrete responses in the actual situations they face. To move toward healing from moral injuries, the caregiver joins the focal conundrums that emerge in the here and now. Naming these, experiencing their power at the felt level of impasse or dilemma, sets the stage to frame them in such a way that contextual creativity and empowering agency might become possible.

The Healing Partnership

How then do we establish partnerships that enable to us to prehend the total gestalt and its innumerable mini-conundrums as a means of healing from moral injury? I will identify the elements of the relational interaction uniquely suited to addressing moral injury, with illustrations from actual situations. What follows blends two approaches that have sat side-by-side in the book up until now. On the one hand, I have developed a structured circular framework for naming, framing, enacting, and revising the results of addressing moral dilemmas and healing moral injuries. This framework is akin to fairly conventional clinical and problem-solving strategies used in a variety of everyday ministry and more specialized professional caregiving contexts. On the other hand, I have emphasized the usefulness of a rather more fluid and innovative process of multiple collaborative conversations within oneself and between oneself and the various contextual social partners implicated in our moral challenges. The first approach is more linear and "expert-focused." The second is more mutual, circular, and "Palaver" focused. In this section and the next chapter I blend the structural and the collaborative. Learning to think and act in this bi-modal way might seem a little complicated and unnecessary at first. But with some discipline and practice the reader should also feel like they have made an important advance in their mental framework and strategic repertoire. In collaborative caregiving, it is essential to keep in mind that healing is discovered through knowledge generated rather than through skills applied. But self-conscious skills can, when strategically employed, provide the social and relational context with the best chance of healing.

Healing the Wounded Soul

After all, I am positing that collaborative caregiving requires discipline and the development of skilled habits of mind!

All helping, both formally and informally, begins with joining the situation and persons in it. To join another requires that we convey a genuine interest in their lives through openness to their truths. It also requires the establishment of a context of safety and unconditional positive regard. Setting the frame for conversations about vulnerable topics requires skill and care. They may take place in formal or informal caregiving situations as well as in many arenas in ordinary living where trust and respect foster such conversation: friends, neighbors, co-workers, fellow churchgoers, salons, and so on. People who gather in these loci of trust and acceptance without judgment have an ordinary context to talk about the moral injury that is a normal but not often disclosed area of their lives. These conditions of acceptance, trust, respect, and curiosity can be engendered in all circumstances ranging from bus-stop chatting to more formal contexts of general and specialized professional care. While the total gestalt of people's lives may not be readily apparent, the most salient mini-conundrums will inevitably surface. This book helps us be more skilled in conversations about moral concerns saturating our everyday encounters.

One of the best ways to establish safety in more formal conversations is to tend to the body. Centering exercises, meditation, focused breathing, and imaginative attunement are means of releasing fear and creating a safe environment. In the discussion of hypnagogy in chapter 6, I demonstrated an example of bodily centering. Tuning into one's body in a relational context can release the impediments to safety and give an empowered sense of personal agency. It mediates a sense of wholeness in the here and the now, releasing us from fears about the future and burdens of the past. It creates a secure base for receiving and containing the emotional dimensions of the moral distress being discussed. It taps into suppressed healthy elements in the psyche to balance out the distressing elements. One can return to the body at any time to re-center and re-empower. Regrouping is a virtue in caregiving.

Once relational trust and contextual safety have been established, more focused strategic elements become relevant. Trust and contextual safety bring us to the point where the conversational collaboration can more clearly name or prehend the total gestalt and identify the focal conundrums ready to be addressed. From here, collaborative exploration allows us to frame the conundrums in positively actionable and contextually creative terms. Moving from actionable framing to engaged action enables a measure of personal agency and hope to become possible. From engaged action, collaborative conversation leads to receiving the outcomes and using them to name, frame, and enact or engage new strategies for the conundrums that come into being.

The fourfold process that mediates healing takes intentional mental effort, evoking new habits of mind and skills for living. In the next chapter I will provide more

– 103 –

detailed guidance about how to name, frame, enact, and revise in actual collaborative endeavors to address moral dilemmas and heal moral injuries. Prior to that, I want to illustrate the features of healing I have discussed in this chapter through a strategic example of healing a moral injury that resulted from abuse by a Nazi prison guard in World War II.

Strategic Example:
Torture, Healing, and Forgiveness

David Chethlahe Paladin was a Native American artist, who was very involved in movements to bring unity and peace throughout the world. He taught at Iliff's summer school in the early 1980s and was a frequent presenter at Iliff conferences and Denver-based events. He blended his artistic gifts with his role as a shaman and moral guide. On many occasions, he shared formative stories from his life and drew spiritual lessons from them. He offered these lessons as potential resources for his listeners. One particular story stands out as an example of healing. It is a difficult story that illustrates how healing is a social and soul-level process of naming, framing, enacting, and revising one's moral history, mediated by forgiveness.

Chethlahe grew up as an alienated youth in Canyon de Chelly, Arizona. He and his cousin were partners in antisocial behaviors and ran away together. They found themselves in San Francisco, California, where they stowed away on a ship to Australia. On that ship was a young German stowaway. The three became friends. When they arrived in Australia, World War II had broken out. Their German friend had to return to Germany. David and his cousin hung around Australia for a while before the United States entered the war. Because they had observed Japan readying for war, they were asked to share information gained while in Australia. This led to David's being employed by the OSS (precursor to the CIA) as a Navajo code talker and later as a spy in Europe. He was arrested as a spy by the Germans, incarcerated in Dachau, and sentenced to death. At Dachau, he met the young German friend from Australia, who had become a prison guard. His friend was now a German officer. He was able to save David from death by arranging for him to be sent to work camps instead of the gas chamber. In the work camp he was brutally tortured, including being nailed to the floor by his feet. At one point the wounds on his legs became gangrenous. He was near death. A Nazi officer visited him secretly during the night. He applied maggots to his infected wound. The officer also forced David to eat raw chicken entrails. David was outraged at these indignities and hated the officer for abusing him.

After the war David was discovered, barely alive, in a train full of dead bodies. He was in a coma for two and a half years. He could walk only with prosthetics. He was full of despair. He went home to say good-bye forever to his family before returning to live out his days in a VA hospital. While at home, his Navajo clan listened to his story and led him, somewhat involuntarily, through a sacred life-review and discernment of the spirit that had captured his life and was holding him back. At that point, the image of the Nazi officer who force-fed him returned. From the depths of his being he said, "All right, I forgive you." He heard the voice of the officer inside him, "Chethlahe, I was trying to keep you alive and those were the only things I could find." These words brought forth a forgotten memory that barged into his mind with life-transforming force. He suddenly recalled an encounter at the Nuremberg trial where he had been asked to witness against this Nazi officer. After his testimony, an unknown person in the court rose and asked the court to consider that perhaps the officer was acting to save David's life, at some risk to his own. The man said that the maggots would have eaten the infection and the chicken entrails provided nourishment to prevent starvation. When the inner voice of forgiveness came together with the guard's words and the words from the bystander in court, David's prior world view was broken apart. "He wept as he released his years of anger and hatred, and resolved never again to hate or condemn another. He forgave himself and others and let all the painful memories go."[5] He did not return to the VA hospital.

David Chethlahe Paladin's remarkable experience could be viewed in many ways, and he seemed to draw various lessons from it. The report I summarized emphasized that healing from soul wounds results from an "unclouding" of our vision in order to restore the soul beauty lost to ourselves and unrecognized in others. It is an invitation for us to see something beautiful that stands hidden in the ugliness of our experiences. In terms of this writing, it means to name our experience in fuller terms, reconnecting with neglected elements, and framing our experience in actionable terms from which release from the past and new moral histories and lessons for living may be derived. For Chethlahe, the core element in this healing process centered on a moral dilemma of whether or not to forgive himself and others for the wounds he carried in his soul because of the egregious immoral acts against him. He chose to move to forgiveness and that changed everything. As his spouse so eloquently stated,

> ... through the process of forgiveness (seeing with new eyes), he had to peel away the soul-clouding emotions of anger and hate from all the events that had captured his spirit, but most especially in the case of the German guard, in order to see that the guard was in fact acting from his inner soul qualities of compassion and love. Through this experience of uncovering and awakening more fully to the beauty of his own essence, Chethlahe was able to see and appreciate the expression of soul beauty in the other. His experience taught him that sometimes, Soul Beauty comes dressed in the strangest garb.[6]

Chapter 8

One of the key outcomes of his healing was for David a new habit of mind toward life, including life's difficulties. David developed the habit of looking for the gift in all circumstances. His physical pain and moral injury had blinded him to the guard's benevolence. He only saw malevolence. He was finally able, through ritual, community support, and new information, to recognize a previously hidden gift. Reframing the guard's actions as benevolence made it possible for him to forgive, or let go of the hatred he carried toward the guard. He was able to release the self-limiting attitudes that had captured his soul. Looking back, he was able to see his torture as a means of seeing the world through new eyes. Based on his transformative healing, he revised his moral history and reset his moral compass. Now he lived with the perpetual expectation of discovering a gift in all circumstances, and he invited us all to do so too.

Not all readers will see much of a gift in this story. They may not see a gift at all. They may see only evil in its rawest form. The conditions or context of the despicable death camps of the Nazi enterprise may brook no redemption by episodic graces. Whatever contextual creativity or punctuated goodness that occurred on the part of the Nazi officer and David's adolescent German roustabout would, for many, be totally eclipsed by the unredeemable evil of the murderous Nazi death machine. I get that. Our moral experiences are part of a whole cloth. They are not internal virtues, values, and attitudes, or even individual actions. They take on meaning and value within the context of the whole of which they are a part. Whatever was a gift to Chethlahe did not diminish or detour the monstrosity of death for millions, or the nearly irreparable diminishment of his own life. To suggest anything else might be considered morally trivial at best and horrendously collusive with unmitigated evil at worst. Put blatantly, one might seriously conclude that it is morally outlandish to find something positive in a Nazi death camp. What is this guy thinking?

Indeed. What am I thinking? I am thinking that small things matter. Light shines in darkness. We do not always see the whole picture of our reality. Contexts always have potential for creative advances, no matter how small or how unapparent at the time. Chethlahe rightly railed against the evil he knew; he held the perpetrators accountable. He also revised his assessment when he saw previously hidden truths and came to a new orientation in his own soul. Evil was strong for him. Evil was stronger than goodness all around him. But there was more going on than what met the eye. For him, something like love—what he termed *soul beauty*—in the Nazi guard meant that he had a new basis for living, recovering, and offering something new and vital to the world. This may not be everything that was needed, or could or should have happened. But it is something. It reflects, however dimly, the radical affirmation that no matter what the situation, "I am as we are, for good or ill."

So, might we not consider that looking for the gift in all circumstances is a foundation for addressing moral dissonance, enduring moral evil, and recovering from moral injury? The reader's answer may be different than mine. But so far the idea and the practice of looking for the gift in every life circumstance has had a beneficial outcome for me and for many I know who practice it. Sometimes the gift is not apparent until much later. Chethlahe's story demonstrates how much time has to pass and how much hard individual and communal soul-work has to be done first. But, sometimes, the gift is there to envision when we simply look around and receive what is offered to us in the ordinary living of our days.

Habits of Mind Exercise: Forgiving the Unforgivable

For Christians, moral living centers forgiveness. Every recital of the Lord's Prayer beseeches God for forgiveness and pledges forgiveness to those who have offended us. The core of forgiveness is to release or to let go of a debt or obligation toward another. Contextual creativity toward the future, including healing from moral injury, proceeds through releasing us from the strictures that hold us in bondage to the past. In David Chethlahe Paladin's case, this meant releasing himself from the self-limitations of hatred and releasing his tormenter from absolute condemnation.

But forgiveness is a complicated moral energy. Sometimes it may be used to avoid accountability and to perpetrate harm. It can keep the abused in an abusive position, without consequence to the offender. In Chethlahe's case, forgiveness was for his own benefit; it was not offered to the guard. Had steps been taken to bring about interpersonal forgiveness or release, other elements would have become necessary. Confession, remorse, apology, and meaningful restitution would come into play.[7] It may or may not have been healing to attempt these steps. And when the actions against David were placed in the context of the Nazi Holocaust, the more morally appropriate course might well have been a decisive withholding of forgiveness. There in fact may be times when it is not moral to forgive the unforgivable.[8]

In David's case, however, he did forgive what at one point in time was not forgivable. Rather than addressing the evil political system of the Nazi tyranny, an unforgivable evil, he forgave a particular individual who rendered help that delivered him from the despicable evil that held him captive. In this case, forgiveness and deliverance from evil were in tandem. In other cases, deliverance from evil may require resistance rather than forgiveness. These are difficult moral choices that may in some circumstances rise to the level of moral dilemma with life or death consequences. Perhaps the gift we look for when facing an impasse about forgiving or not forgiving is the clarity and moral courage that emerge as we discern the right path to take.[9]

As a habit of mind exercise, write down your inner dialogue as you read through this chapter on healing. What interested, excited, or challenged you about it? What light did it throw on your own experience? Paying special attention to David Paladin's account of healing from moral injury through forgiveness, what seemed new for you? What can you do with this? Where would it help you to look for the gift in the circumstances of your life? Are you in conversations with others with whom David's experience would be helpful? How might you introduce it meaningfully? Finally, what can you take away from this chapter that will be fruitful for setting and following your moral compass? What will you leave behind? Why?

To summarize and conclude, healing the soul's moral wounds is both a personal and social endeavor. Pastoral and communal guidance takes the initiative of joining the painful terrain of moral pain and creates a safe place to grieve the multiple losses brought on by the wounding, and to name, frame, enact, and revise the wounding events. Forgiveness is an ambiguous resource by which to become free of the bondage of the past and look for gifts previously unrecognized. Healing is best realized when the body feels whole and positively connected to the soul. Other markers of healing are clarity about moral responsibility; the capacity for self-regulation; a positive relationship to the past, present, and future; nurturing relational patterns; and a basic sense of safety in the world. In the next chapter we will explore more precise micro-strategies for engaging one another in collaborative healing conversations and activities.

For Further Reading

Buzzell, Linda, and Craig Chalquist. *Ecotherapy: Healing with Nature in Mind.* San Francisco: Sierra Club Books, 2009.

Collins-Hughes, Laura. "Using Shakespeare to Ease the Trauma of War." *New York Times*, March 9, 2017. www.nytimes.com/2017/03/09/theater/shakespeare-military-stephan-wolfert-cry-havoc.html.

Lerner, Harriet. *Why Won't You Apologize? Healing Big Betrayals and Everyday Hurts.* New York: Simon and Schuster, 2017.

Suchocki, Marjorie Hewitt. *The Fall to Violence: Original Sin in Relational Theology.* New York: Continuum, 2004.

CHAPTER 9

Healing Collaborations

The heart of this book is about collaborative conversations that enhance moral decisions and heal moral injuries. What follows are particular conversational skills for the caregiver to learn and employ in conversations with themselves and with those whom they serve. The interactions I portray are suggestive rather than prescriptive. The caregiver or reader will select from them and add to them as the situation unfolds.

The conversational strategies I present will be illustrated by actual situations as examples but not as templates or models for other forms of moral injuries. While there will be transferable insights and behaviors, each moral injury is born by its own dynamics and context. I will link personal, relational, and social-cultural elements as much as possible. And I will attempt to show how the contextually creative collaborative strategies of naming, framing, engaging, and revising our moral histories may enhance resiliency and promote healing. Though the focus is on healing moral injury, this process can also be employed to address moral dissonance and various moral dilemmas. The form of the discourse is an imaginative collaborative conversation, initiated by the caregiver. The other side of the conversation is not set forth. The reader is invited to enter and complete the conversation imaginatively, and to adapt it to their inner dialogue as well as to the conversations they are having with others. In a word, this chapter is a lengthy habits of mind exercise.

Let me remind the reader that I am offering a process that anyone can follow. One does not need to be a pastoral care or psychotherapeutic specialist to employ these strategies for engaging oneself and others in the arena of moral pain. I am trying to normalize the difficult. When we sort pain and pain-bearers into special categories, we isolate the pain-bearer and valorize the caregiver. We create stigma and we deplete the regenerative power of our relationships, communities, and cultural assets. By respectful listening and genuine interest, the caregiver can understand the particular social situation, the various loyalties, and the array of moral meanings compelling attention and a contextually creative response. And while sometimes special expertise and sophisticated technologies are required, they are best regarded as supplemental to organic natural processes. Lateral mutuality is an overlooked or underdeveloped human resource. We keep looking for experts and authorities to see us through, and sometimes they do emerge and set us free. But we cannot overlook the vital energies embedded in our daily practices and surrounding world. Palaver palliates. Dialogue diagnoses. Collaboration cures. Lamentation liberates. Memorializing motivates.

Naming the Moral Injury

The power to name one's moral situation is one of our most significant human powers. The Genesis story of our archetypal moral forebears portrays the search for the knowledge of good and evil as our core human situation, morally speaking. And, to be sure, the compulsion to name our moral situation is fraught with danger and cost, as well as holding potential for advancement and improvement. Failure to name the moral dimensions of our humanity is to refuse our humanity under God, and naming our dilemmas and injuries is in itself a moral act. The collaborative process of naming is also a part of living out the co-humanity of our divine creation: it is not good that men and women should be alone but that we should face our perils and possibilities together. After all, "I am as we are." Sharing the naming process helps us to bear the debilitating aspects of what is there to embrace, as well as to heal.

How we name what we are struggling to bear is important. There are two very nonproductive ways to name them. First, we can name them as fatal flaws before which we are helpless and overwhelmed. This is the "Woe is me!" mindset, which holds us back. Second, we can name the moral dilemmas and injuries from a judgmental and condemnatory standpoint. This is the "I am lost beyond hope" mindset, which also holds us back. When named these ways, the bearer of moral challenges and moral failures will feel smaller, isolated, ashamed, and, most likely, reinjured. That is, we must be very careful not to inflict moral injury in the conversations we initiate or the language frames we use to try to relieve or resolve moral injury. We must always "mind the righteousness gap"! Self-awareness and self-correction about the meta-message we give off is always required when we enter the tough and tender territory of moral struggles.

Rather than reinforcing helplessness, judgmentalism, and moralistic "shoulds" and "oughts," the collaborative companion brings an affirmation of courage to confront these difficult matters and offers an invitation to grow and heal from them.

Naming the courage to confront our conundrums as a moral virtue in itself reduces the helplessness, shame, guilt, and isolation that so often attend moral injury. If I think of myself as courageous, I can find a measure of strength to address my difficulties. Moreover, if I understand that I am not alone, I can begin to feel hopeful. If I see that all humans struggle with excruciating moral challenges, I can begin to feel less stigmatized and more creatively engaged in finding ways to move forward. Then I am reminded that no matter what our situation, there always remains a level of contextual creativity for new forms of agency.

Naming, therefore, is a co-creative process that joins and enhances the natural human resiliency necessary to bear and overcome traumatic challenges. It emphasizes strength and renewal over impairment and failure. The collaborative questions I suggest below are means of assisting the two-way conversation. They create the Palaver, the place of engagement for understanding and change. Conversation partners who do best are those who develop the habit of mind that recognizes that the collaborative questions emerging in the interaction are not diagnostic questions. This is especially hard for therapists, who have learned a variety of treatment modes based on diagnostic criteria. It is equally hard for ministers, whether therapeutically trained or not. All of us have internalized schema that assess, explain, and guide our actions for the welfare of others. To suspend these schema, or, better, to use them imaginatively to explore rather than to diagnose and treat is a major shift that to some readers may be neither desirable nor possible. But those willing to attempt this approach will expand their caregiving repertoire. Asking caregivers to suspend the diagnostic-treatment mindset is not to disparage that model of care. Certainly, there is often a very significant positive result from doing things in the "diagnosis-treatment" mode of rendering assistance, but it is only one way of doing things. It would be my hope that the caregiver would become multi-modal rather than confined by a mono-modal of assisting with the pain and challenge of moral injury and moral courage.

Curiosity, understood as the sympathetic interest in the other, is at the center of the caregiving conversations I am proposing. Curiosity is the vital medium for naming collaboratively the painful conundrums we face—whether these conundrums take the form of moral dissonance, moral dilemma, or moral injury. Curiosity embodies a genuine desire to prehend—to feel, know, and understand—what is going on in the total gestalt of another and in the emerging relationship between us. Open-minded and appreciative curiosity is the mode of relationality here. Sharing one's inner dialogue about what is interesting and exciting, or even challenging, from what I am hearing is the means of normalizing the abnormal and creating a new bond of care and belonging between two people. All parties in the conversation have mutual responsibilities for maintaining and strengthening the bond that comes into place between them. But neither is the expert over the other's experience, knowledge, and decisions. Through curious interest and mutual pursuit of the salient, new knowledge is generated and new solutions come into view; contextually creative outcomes are discovered rather than applied.

The temptation at this point is to say, "Well and good, so far. I can do this. But at a certain point this could just keep you unfocused and going around in circles. I do not think it is helpful to chase every rabbit that can come up in what you call this collaborative curious co-creative process. We do have to focus and figure out what to do with what we are discovering. And, to be blunt, sometimes the trained expert does know best what can and cannot be helpful to others." I take this as a fair voice from common sense and professional convention. My answer at this point is to wait and see where this dialogue leads. Naming is just one element of a larger enterprise. As we proceed, we will add framing, enacting, and revising what comes into being. There may yet be a time for "treatment" but the data set we need to start "treatment planning" is a few pages away.

In what follows, I would like to suggest some collaborative questions and conversational starting points to help name the moral wound for which assistance is invited. Of course, these are adaptable to the situation. The best questions arise from curiosity in the moment rather than from a checklist lifted from a book. There is no particular order to this list, though the first two questions are good starting points. In the actual conversation, it is better to proceed from what arises in response to the questions than to use them as a data-gathering interview guide. Staying tuned to and then sharing what excites, interests, or confounds my inner dialogue will shape the most productive change. Above all, it would be a mistake to use all the questions that follow below as an intake guide for gathering information before determining what treatment to pursue. In actual experience, moral conundrums are small and focused. They emerge quickly in conversations. Adapting the questions from the "wide net" to the "micro-screen" will take alertness and skill. The interaction around the conversation is the "treatment plan." Approaching moral difficulties through this mode of engagement may or may not lead to tried and true trails out of the morass. But it has a very good chance of creating new trails and bridges—and maybe even an airfield or train station—by which to move to a better place.

Now, here are some concrete suggestions for working together to name the moral situation concerning the careseeker. Finally, we are joining the Palaver! I am presenting these as imaginary conversational starting points initiated by the caregiver. Of course, in actual practice the interaction is much more mutually dynamic. I invite the reader to listen in and join this one-sided conversation.

Collaborative Questions for Naming Moral Injury

I am glad that you indicated you are struggling. It takes a lot of courage to share something as personal as moral challenges. But sharing them is the best way I know to bear them and move beyond them. I am curious about your core concerns right now. Would you feel comfortable sharing your thoughts? I will share mine as we go along, too, if that is okay with you. I would like to learn more about the moral concerns you are experiencing, especially those that you have strong feelings about.

Let me also ask a very specific question. We are here to talk about moral injuries to the soul, about soul wounds. What is the soul for you? How would you describe your soul? What kind of shape is it in?

As you tell me these things, I am finding myself getting a bit tense and a little sad inside. These are very moving and engaging matters. Are you aware of what you are feeling in your body as we talk? When our bodies and emotions come into play, we are really coming close to our souls. We want to stay at the emotional level, but not be unnecessarily overwhelmed by emotions. Maybe we can take a few minutes to relax, breathe deeply, and connect with some good energy to calm us down and take some of the stress out of things right now. In addition to making the stressful emotions a little less dominant, we want to bring into play some of the other emotions you feel good about. Some people don't find this very helpful, but others do. Would you be willing to give it a try and see what happens? Let me take you through a brief centering exercise. We can return to this briefly at any time to re-center ourselves. Let me know when you want to do so.[1]

How would you describe the concern that is bothering you? Can you tell me about what most concerns you about it? How is it affecting your life? What have you done to try to address it? What helped and what didn't help? Are there hidden feelings about it that should be surfaced? [Note: One would not pile these questions

on top of one another all at once; they are a sequence that might be
expected to emerge in the conversation.]

Can you name what is most at stake for you in this moral concern
or moral injury? Or if the dilemma you are facing isn't handled in
the best way, what will be the consequences? What will that mean
for you? Are there pressures on you from others not to address
this or change?

What did it cost, or take away? Can you share the losses it brought
into your life? How are they affecting you?

What did this injury not take from you? What remains that you are
glad about or proud of? What does that say about you? How might
the strength that is left over be a resource for you down the trail?
Can you look for the gift for you that might be hidden here?

How might what is left help you face with strength the moral challenges before you now? What happens when you emphasize your
assets rather than your deficiencies when you think about your
dilemma and your injury?

Framing the Moral Injury in Actionable Terms

Once the conversation to name the moral concern and gather some of its dimensions has occurred, it is critical to frame the problem in actionable terms. Contextual
creativity requires agency, or action. Action is mental as well as behavioral. Action
allows for correction and healing. Framing as actionable moves the concern from the
internal space of the person or group, to the larger environment where empowered
responses become possible. Briefly put, now that we have named the moral concern
as normal, we are framing it as actionable. Naming alone paralyzes; framing as actionable empowers change. Here are some questions and suggestions about how to
frame what has been named as a moral concern into collaboratively infused actionable items. More conventionally stated, this is the beginning of some goal-setting to
structure actions necessary for healing the past and enhancing the well-being of the
group or individual in the future.

Collaborative Questions for Framing Moral Injury

Now that we have discovered where you are caught in your dilemma and injury, we can begin to imagine some ways to talk about this in terms of realizing your values and accomplishing your goals. Let us see if we can work with what you said was the strength that remains available to you. Your strengths will help us to frame something positive that you would like to see happen now. Does something come to mind? We can begin small! We will do this over and over. Remember, right now we want to focus on what is left, not what is lost. We need to release thoughts from the past and focus on the here and now. We also do not want to consider whether what we are framing can be accomplished in the future. [That is, do not follow your framing with the thought, "But I have done that and it didn't do any good."] Anything goes right now. Realistic strategies come later once we have framed what you want in terms of your true desires. Is something coming up that seems interesting or exciting to you to put on the table? What is flowing for you now? What is your body saying? Can you envision what you would like to have happen?

Let us keep working at this. The main thing right now is to frame what you would like to have happen in doable terms. If we cannot make a beginning here, your burden will stay in place. So, let us be sure we are framing this in realistically beneficial terms so you will see an end-result worth moving toward. We want the end point to be doable, but also beneficial. If it is framed properly, it is predictably doable. If framed improperly it is either not worth doing or not doable at all. What really is at stake for you here; and how do we formulate actions you can take that will be pleasant, easy, and beneficial for you right now? What do you imagine you can do right away to feel good about? Do you think you can frame your next steps in terms that (1) you desire, and (2) you can begin to act to bring about?

I have been talking about making this pleasant, easy, and beneficial right now. I know that sounds too simple. I don't mean it to be. This is really hard. Like driving a car, it takes some getting used to. So, let me ask you this. What would you say is the optimal level of discomfort that you need to help you change? Too much discomfort will make you avoid change. Too little will make change seem trivial or unnecessary. How do we work to regulate your discomfort level so it is a positive tool for us? I am really eager to hear what you think about this. What would make your next steps productively more difficult?

I am also curious about your thoughts about willpower. Some think that willpower is required to change. I do not agree with that. To change, I think we need to be clear about what we really want, about our true intentions and goals. But willpower usually means we are trying to force ourselves to do something that we really cannot admit that we do not want to do. So, are you framing these goals in terms of what you think you "ought" to be doing or in terms of what you really want? Can you frame this in terms of doing something now that will bring you pleasure rather than force you to fight against your true desires? Can you accept good feelings toward yourself when you do good things?

Because moral concerns are so fraught with shame, guilt, and a sense of failure we would be remiss not to discuss the guilt and shame elements at the heart of your moral concern. Some people think that guilt and shame are different. They are, no doubt, different theoretically and psychologically. But I have found them to be somewhat co-incidental in the lived experience of moral concern and moral injury. Therefore, I would like us to use the terms interchangeably at this point in our conversation. We have named the shame and guilt you carry from the moral conundrum we are discussing. That takes courage and shows true strength.

But we must be careful to assess how shame and guilt pertain. First, they pertain to assessing one's own actions. I feel shame and guilt for things I have done or not done. Second, they pertain to what someone else has done to me. I feel shame and guilt because I have lost something or have been violated. I may feel shame and guilt because I think I should have been able to prevent this. Third, I feel shame and guilt because of what I did or didn't do to heal from the wounds others have caused in my life. To make guilt and shame productive in your life we must name clearly how they link to your agency, and then frame your understanding in actionable terms rather than letting them remain only as feelings. We must move shame and guilt from bodily emotions to bodily behaviors. Making this move will neutralize the isolation, paralysis, and self-condemnation that the shame and guilt dimensions of moral injury leave inside us. It will also help us prevent the danger of moral outrage dominating our minds rather than empowering strategic actions on behalf of our best interests.[2] It is very important that we not just name the outrage, but that we channel its energies into doable and productive behaviors toward those who harm us.

It is also very important to explore what you have and have not done so far with these feelings. It is crucial to name something that you have done, or continue to do, that keeps you stuck in this dilemma. Are there some ways that you are morally injuring yourself by what you are doing or not doing? I know that these questions may move us beyond your optimal level of discomfort, and we may need to calm down the body and emotions through re-centering. But I am really curious to hear how you think about this. And I am really curious to think with you about how you might reframe your responses to your original injury in terms that are more beneficial for you. What do you think? So, when I say these things what comes to mind? What kind of inner dialogue does it set off for you? I am very curious to hear your thoughts.

Before we move on to strategic engagement, let me summarize where we are. You have named your core moral concerns and have begun to frame them in actionable terms beneficial to yourself. How has that been for you? Are other things coming to mind we should talk about? Let me share my main insights about what you have said and tell you what is exciting and challenging to me, and what I remain curious about. Then let us explore some ways you might reengage your life in light of these new intentions and goals.

Enacting Moral Change

Now you and the careseeker know what you really want to have happen next. You have helped frame these desires in terms that will help employ their true strengths to fulfill them.

Chapter 9

Collaborative Questions for Enacting Moral Change

How might you use collaborative questions and conversations to continue to engage your situation productively? I call this "strategic enactment" of your moral challenges. It is where you draw on your strengths and desires to change your relation to the past and create a new future through trial and error enactments of the burgeoning new vision for your life.

I find it helpful to begin with the imagination. Let's use your imagination to consider what steps you might take to change things for the better. Imaginative rehearsal is one of the greatest resources we have for seeing what we really want and need to do. Imaginative rehearsal provides a user-friendly way to realize your intentions on the ground. Sometimes the dreams you have at night will give you a clue about how to proceed (or not to proceed). Dreams can provide both direction and energy to move to a new place. They often convey a sense of divine presence and power. Sometimes the subliminal nighttime conversations we have with ourselves show us what we need to do, and can do. If we listen to these, it becomes relatively easy to take new actions.[3]

So, what comes to mind for you as you hear this? What can you imagine doing next? What do you imagine will come into place to help you overcome or address any opposition or impediments to actually doing what you imagine? Do you have any sense of divine guidance emerging for you? Are any dreams or nighttime musings giving you clues about what to do next?

It may be helpful to remember the hypnagogic exercise for resolving impasses, dilemmas, and conundrums.[4] Is there a block—a logjam—that you can think of and see if your mind leads you to formulate a beneficial action?

I remember a student in one of my classes who was dreading going to see her mother on holiday break. She said her mother never listened. She was always critical and telling her what to do. They ended up fighting. She always returned to school wishing she had not gone home. The dissonance between her and her mother was diminishing her soul and impairing her agency. The mother-daughter relationship was also wounded. The class asked her to formulate this visit in different terms: "Rather than figuring how not to fight with your mother, or how to win the fights, why not ask your mother for some advice that would really help you if she were able to give it?" This framing stopped her in her tracks. She went back and forth in her mind between fighting with Mom and finding wisdom from Mom. Hypnagogy helped her to decide to seek Mom's wisdom rather than trying to avoid fighting. She re-framed her relationship with her mother as ally rather than ad-versary. She realized that both she and her Mom were single par-ents and that she really needed some advice how to do a better job with her daughter. When she returned from the visit, she told the class that her Mom not only gave very helpful advice, but that they did not fight once. In fact, they now were talking by phone as adult-to-adult a couple times a week. The class told her how good it was that her mother could actually change after all these years of rigidity.

Does this scenario suggest any possibilities for you? Shall we hyp-nagogue together?

Brett Litz and his colleagues incorporate an imaginative exercise you might want to consider. They suggest that persons carry two types of moral injuries: betrayal-based moral injury due to the loss of friends and comrades, and perpetuation-based moral injury due to their own moral conflicts about their actions in war. To find relief, Litz and his colleagues lead the careseeker in an imaginative conversation with the parties they feel they failed. In the case of a lost friend or comrade, they suggest talking to them and hearing their words back to you. Usually, those friends will offer acceptance and encouragement to live well. In the case of perpetuation-based moral injury, they suggest an imaginative conversation with a safe, accepting moral authority such as a priest, pastor, or other spiri-tual leader. Usually, they will find relief from self-condemnation and paralyzing shame.[5] I know that we are doing some of those things here together, but I wonder what you think of adding this to your repertoire. What is your inner dialogue when you hear this?

To act as an efficacious agent based on our reframed goals sometimes requires us to change our moral position in relation to others or the circumstances. We have four variable positions operating in our moral situations: we are moral movers, moral opposers, moral joiners, and moral observers.[6] The college student and her mom who were mentioned above were locked into a mover-opposition dyad. It was futile and hurtful. When the daughter changed her moral position to move toward joining her mother—rather than opposing her—something radically new happened. The discourse was framed in more beneficial and actionable moral terms (how to be a good single parent) rather than staying stuck in a conflict over whose sense of the right thing should prevail. Is there a situation where you might consider changing your moral position to build the discourse around something different, but equally true and important for you? Let us explore this. Is there someone you should join rather than oppose? Or oppose whom you have joined? What other things come to mind about becoming more flexible with your moral standpoint?

The conversation we are now having about enacting change focuses on concrete things you can put into action. We are involved in collaboratively empowered problem-solving. We do not know when we start talking what you will discover and act on. I find it helpful to brainstorm about possible strategies to meet your goals. What comes to mind when I say this?

Following from brainstorming, let us see what small steps can be taken now. Let us identify some doable actions to start with. This is the beginning of the "trial and error" aspects of change. What needs to be your focus now? With whom do you need to talk? What do you need to say no to? What thoughts do you need to stop or let go of? Be careful not to get into a "yes...but" mindset. We need to stay grounded in the power of your mind and body working together to feel a "yes, we can do this" mindset. From there you can try out something new. What do you think?

Do you think that we can begin to formulate an action plan in three parts? We can think in terms of immediate, short-term, and long-term actions. Imagine yourself as beginning a new dance, or taking dance lessons. What comes first? When you imagine choreograph-ing your moves, what do you see? Who are your dance partners? Where is your dance floor? Remember, all this can change as we gather information from what happens when you change-up the dance.

Is this a good time to pause and ask for divine assistance? Do you need direction? Do you need inspiration? Do you need divine em-powerment? Are you praying about this? How do you pray? What happens to you when you pray? Is this the time to recognize the spiritual strengths that are emerging as you engage this chal-lenge? What comes to mind as we look at these spiritual dimen-sions? How can they be helpful now? Does your guilt block access to divine assistance? What happens inside when I bring up the question of the divine?

It is really important that you realize that you are not alone. One of the strong features of moral trauma and moral shame is its power to isolate. It makes us want to hide. When we hide we feel safer, but, really, we end up feeling all the more helpless and alone. Now is the time for you to find simpatico partnerships to support and guide you. This is risky. Some may fail to understand you. Often your partners will feel a need to tell you what to do, or they might hijack your story with theirs. But when you step out to broaden trustworthy networks, you are well on the way to change. Remem-ber, we are not trying to make you a self-reliant automaton, cut off from vital relationships. We are working to embrace the goodness in the human community that affirms "I am as we are." You will be better when the vitality of the human community offsets the virulence and injury that have come into your life. You can help educate them about what really helps you.

To begin this immersion into simpatico partnerships, tell me about your closest friends. How might they be employed to help you with this next step? Are there support and therapy groups for what you are struggling with? For example, veterans talking with veterans and women talking with women can make all the differ-ence. Remember, this is not all about you. If you embed yourself in these groups you will help others too. Since "I am as we are," there is something healing in helping others. Are there advocacy groups who need your resources and who can help you? What about Bible studies and prayer groups? When you can share your pain in a trustworthy context, you can bear it better. When you share your hopes and goals, others will help you fulfill them. Would a good therapist or spiritual counselor be of value to you? What do you think about all this? What was your inner dialogue? What seems promising? Let us build on that and ignore the rest for now.

At this point in the conversation, it is not uncommon for people to realize that they need to reassess their moral compasses and spiritual meanings. All of us have internalized moral values and spiritual convictions that no longer serve us very well. In fact, they can be part of the problem. Professor Carrie Doehring says that we often get stuck spiritually and morally because the theologies and moral values that became embedded in our psyches need to be recognized and updated through more deliberative processes when they no longer serve in life-giving ways.[7]

Can we look more deeply at how your values and spiritual meanings might be contributing to your difficulties now? Maybe they need to be reengaged and revised for you to have the inner resources and the moral support you need for what you are facing.[8] What do you think?

Now that we have some directions in place and a broader network to trust, I wonder if it is time to introduce forgiveness for your consideration. Forgiveness is a very tricky and potentially harmful category. Sometimes the way people push the idea of forgiveness actually causes moral dissonance and moral harm. But forgiveness can be an essential dimension of moral healing and a means to find genuine freedom from moral burdens that bring us down.

Can you share your immediate reaction when I suggested that forgiveness might help you now? What is your inner dialogue about forgiving and forgiveness? I would especially like to hear where you locate forgiveness: toward yourself, to or from others, to or from God, or to or from your nation?

Let me say why I think it may be helpful, either now or later, to let forgiveness become a resource for your healing. Forgiveness

fundamentally means "to release" or "to let go of." It is not just a religious category, but an everyday category. If I tell you that I accept
your apology for not paying back the one hundred dollars I lent
you, and tell you that you do not have to repay me at all, I have let
go, released, or forgiven that obligation. You are free of it. And so
am I. We can move on. That is all there is to it. And I can forgive or
let go of the debt you owe me whether you apologize or not. I can
say, "Diane, I am going to forget about that one hundred dollars
you owe me. You are free and clear. Bygones are bygones."

So, is there something you need to forgive in order to move on?
Something you need to forgive yourself for? Something you need
to forgive someone else for? Let's make a list and take them one
by one.

We just looked at the relatively easy part of forgiveness: forgiving
self and others. It takes courage and strength to do this, and to
heal the hurt, guilt, shame, and resentment that may remain even
though forgiveness is heartfelt. But it is much harder to ask for
forgiveness from someone we have harmed who may not want
to hear from us. They may find our reaching out to be offensive,
and our request for forgiveness a moral affront to the gravity of
the harm we caused or contributed to. In fact, it may be morally
harmful to us and to them to even approach them about forgiveness. In these cases, forgiveness may become possible only after
some other things happen first. Sometimes forgiveness requires
many detours: finding mediators, taking corrective action, public
apology, social change, legal action, advocacy, and meaningful restitution. To make forgiveness emotionally and relationally real we
have to honor the offended party's moral obligation to sometimes
not forgive us. In these cases, we may have to find ways to live
on the opposite sides of an uncrossable moral chasm in ways that
do not cause additional injury. To be sure, we have also to recognize that sometimes chasms are bridged. They may be flown over.
There might be trails around or through them. But sometimes they
are permanently stuck in place as monuments to the cataclysmic
wounds that we have carved into history. The question then becomes how do we live as well as possible in the face of these ongoing gaps?

Do you have situations like that? What avenues lie before you to engage those who do not want to consider your remorse and offer you forgiveness? What would moral strength look like to help you bear the unforgivable actions you have done or contributed to?

Another difficulty is finding forgiveness from someone who has died. This can be a complicated process, with ambiguous results. But writing letters, engaging imaginative conversation with the deceased, and visiting the grave site can be helpful. If their relatives are open to it, forgiveness might be mediated over time. Do any of these ideas resonate with you?

Before we wrap up, I want to throw a little dissonance into the conversation. Here is my question. "What is funny in your situation?" I am asking if there is something amusing in all this that we should think about. Humor is an everyday form of transcendence. It allows us to see our situation with new eyes. Humor is a tool of agency. It can also be a tool of anxiety, power, and shame, so let's be careful here. So, what strikes you as funny here? Is there anything in yourself that makes you laugh? Anything in this situation?

What does it say about you that you can find humor in these serious matters? How can what you think is funny help you engage more freely what you are setting off to engage? How might the humor we are identifying here be a resource of engagement and collaboration for you?

What stands out from your inner dialogue about these concrete strategies we have explored to engage the moral challenges you are dealing with? Where do they lead you? What will you do? Remember, you are not alone as you try these out. I am in your head; so are your friends and others. Be sure to keep the conversations going. They will be most helpful to keep framing your actions in terms of your strengths and positive agency. Stop the self-condemnation chatter. Be aware of your body-self and move from bodily stress to body fluidity. Keep telling yourself that you do not need to do everything at once. Small steps can leave big footprints!

Revising Moral Histories

We will now leave the naming, framing, and enacting elements of moral healing and turn to the revising phase. Remember, all of these elements work together and blend into one another. Remind the careseeker to remain alive to their inner dialogue, especially through body-talk, which will be the best way stay rooted in their core strengths.

Collaborative Questions for Revising Moral Histories

Up until now we have focused on the power of personal and social agency in naming, framing, and engaging your moral challenges. In this final phase, we emphasize receptive power as the capacity to be influenced by what happens as a result of our actions. Put another way, we have two forms of power available to us. The first form of power is agential power—the capacity to influence and initiate. The second form of power is receptive power—the capacity to be influenced and changed by what comes to us. The capacity to revise our moral histories comes from our inherent human ability to be receptive agents of power as well as initiating agents of power. In this phase of the conversation, we want to expand your capacity to change and heal through receiving the positive outcomes of what you have been doing to address your moral dilemmas and injuries. Without the capacity or power to receive new influences, there is no power to change or revise our lives. But receiving something is very difficult, and takes moral courage too. The capacity to accept good things resulting from our efforts is especially hard when we feel like we do not deserve good things because we are morally "bad" people or have done unforgivable things. This is not only difficult for people who have actually done bad things, but can also be true for those who were the recipients of harm by others. That is why receiving the positive outcomes of our efforts is so difficult.

It is a spiritual discipline to receive life's positive gifts and to reclaim the blessings of goodness meant for us. Habits of thought and practice have an enduring quality. Changing them requires new habits of mind and new exercises of power. The conversation we are about to have will try to expand your capacity to affirm and embody the changes you are trying to make in your life now. What is your inner dialogue when you hear this? What excites you about it? What are you curious about? Does anything challenge you?

The second thing to do now is to clearly name the gains or positive outcomes that have come from what you have been attempting. It is important that you make these "yours." I call this "anchoring your gains." Putting an anchor down holds your boat in place where you want it to be. Some people develop little mental tricks to help them anchor their gains and connect with their strengths. For example, one person I know felt really good because she decided not to argue with her mother, but to ask her mother questions that she really thought that her mother could answer helpfully. She anchored this memory by looking at a picture of her mother. You might anchor your own positive thoughts and memories by touching your heart. When you touch your heart, you will be taken back into the positive experience that you want to hold on to. You can infuse your body and mind with the good feelings. Another person I know has found that "stopping thoughts" was very productive for them. They began to recognize how their mind automatically wandered into swamps of negative memories or failed efforts. Rather than slogging through this territory, they just stopped thinking about it. To anchor the capacity to stop nonproductive thoughts, they found that looking up, changing where their eyes focused, did the trick. They looked up to the art on the walls of the room, or to the treetops visible through the windows. The simple act of moving their focus from down to up changed the moral and spiritual landscape of their inner world.

Can we work together to see what gains you made and find some ways to anchor them? That way they will always be under your control. If you receive these gains now, they will be part of your body and soul and always available to you as your core strength. What comes to mind? What are the main changes you see in your thinking and actions? What is your inner dialogue about these changes? How will you employ these gains in what you do next?

Is there a way to anchor them in your body and mind so you can return to them whenever you need to?

As we begin to shift our attention from receiving the results of your efforts to naming the new conundrums now coming into focus, it will be valuable to talk about some cautions. The first caution is not to lose sight of the pressure of the past to negate or minimize your efforts. You will find yourself vulnerable to the "yes…but" messages that always debilitate. "Yes, I began to forgive myself and change my behaviors, but that doesn't take away the harm I caused." When this happens, what can you do? Remember thought-stopping. You can also fight back by reframing the discounting messages into positive messages about yourself. Say instead, "I did cause harm to others, and I am trusting that I and others can heal from these wounds through forgiveness and changed behavior. I am taking one step at a time!" Be especially careful not to fall into self-blame.

A second caution is to be realistic about the "remainders," or the "leftovers." We are working on matters that do not have full and permanent solutions. There will always be more to do, or better ways to do it. And we may temporarily increase harm or feel more pain as we try to heal injury. No matter how much we attempt and how much we accomplish, there are huge forces within us and around us that resist our efforts. It is critical not to expect a perfect solution to the moral morasses we endure. The "remainders," "gaps," and "leftovers" can be negotiated if we name and normalize them. It makes a huge difference if we are able to embrace the gaps rather than being pulled into them.

My best image of being realistic in the face of ongoing brokenness is the spider's web. A web by nature has gaps. And sometimes the web becomes torn. Between the gaps necessary for there to be a web in the first place and the web's "tornness by life," there remains permanent imperfection and unbridgeable gulfs. But the spider lives and finds ways to negotiate, repair, and find food in what remains of the web. There are strong strands holding the tattered and porous web together, yielding a basis for the spider to live and even thrive. These threads provide trails and footholds to move around the web's gaps and tears. They render the web strong and useful. So, where is your web still torn, even after your efforts to repair and heal? What are the strands in the web that remain that can give you life and keep you going? What are the resources still available to repair the web and live well in spite of its gaps and tears? Can you make this concrete in your situation?

We have now come full circle in the process of resolving moral conundrums through the contextually creative activity of naming, framing, enacting, and revising the consequences of our moral actions. It is now fitting to "rinse and repeat" this circular dance. How would you name the challenges coming to light now? How do you think of them? How might you frame them in terms of actionable goals? What strategies might you start with to engage challenges in the light of your goals? What outcomes to you hope to see, and how will you receive them into your life if they do come about?

Before moving on to illustrate moral healing through the eyes of a veteran, I want to conclude this section with two thoughts for the reader. First, I recognize that this elaborate schema will be meaningless and unusable to some. Translating a process from a book to lived experience is fraught with many levels of frustration and futility. I recognize this, and I am sympathetic.

Second, I recognize that even for those who can move from a book to lived experience, the process I am outlining in this book may not be compatible with the mindset and experience of some to whom it will be introduced. Mine is a relationally intensive and intrapsychically focused approach. My approach will be helpful to a degree with those who are comfortable accessing their internal dynamics and who are comfortable with interpersonal self-disclosures. But for those who are more behaviorally oriented and communally embedded, this might seem like way too much naval-gazing and intersubjective muddling. If that is the case, my advice is to focus the conversation on behaviors and social processes, expanding the comfort level in discussing these elements rather than favoring the intrapsychic and interpersonal elements with which I tend to be comfortable. Find your way to advocacy and support groups to change the circumstances you are trying to overcome. After all, the point is for the care provider to be curious and excited about the person they are helping, and to let this curiosity and excitement pave the way. It is not about imposing a preset model on to another's life. But with some attentive discipline, collaborative engagement of whatever is presented to us by another will begin to create some of the conditions necessary for beneficial change.

Strategic Example:
A Veteran Struggles to Heal

Gary wants to help others by sharing his story of healing his soul wounds from two combat deployments in Afghanistan. His story is used with his permission, but his identity and some major facts of his history are thoroughly disguised. I came into Gary's world through a pastoral counseling colleague I have known and respected for several decades, whom I'll refer to here as Ellen. As I was sharing with her the main features of this book, she described her pastoral counseling with Gary. Her portrayal of their work together spoke to the heart of collaborative engagement around moral injuries. Ellen has reviewed, edited, and approved this presentation. Though her work with Gary takes place in a pastoral counseling therapeutic context, the conversations reported below are readily within the scope of a chaplain, spiritual-director, life-coach, parish-based pastor, and close friend. I will tie the pastoral conversation to the earlier presentation of collaboratively creative engagement of soul wounds through the process of naming, framing, enacting, and revising one's painful moral history.

Gary sought Ellen's help through the advice of a mutual friend. Gary is thirty years old. For a little over two years, he has received treatment for his PTSD through various VA programs such as group and individual therapy and various drug protocols. And while these have been helpful, he continues to label himself as defective. He is not able to sustain significant relationships. He is particularly upset that he lost a job that he loved and was good at because those who promised to write references for him never followed through. He has not found suitable employment and lives on the largesse of a generous family member. A second wound is the abandonment of his marriage by his wife. For reasons of which I am unclear, she decided to "just up and leave" the marriage, leaving him bereft and lost. He lives with a pervasive sense that he is defective because he cannot get his life going the way he wants it to go.

These post-deployment challenges are attributed to outcomes of the stresses, traumas, and losses that he experienced while in Afghanistan. He lives with considerable flashbacks, anxiety, and depression. When Ellen asked about his combat experiences, he shared many examples of losing friends and comrades in combat and the terrible effects of seeing civilian men, women, and children brutally killed. These were acute personal losses and morally horrifying human events. He could not shake their pervasive residence in his mind. He carries self-blame for not being able to move beyond these traumatic losses and their disruption of his soul. In terms of traumatic loss and moral injury, Gary lives with a dislocated consciousness characterized by time out of place, defective agency, and a body questing for intimacy and significant

– 129 –

relationships. Grief and loss associated with trauma and life events paralyze and diminish him.

After about six sessions, Ellen realized that their conversations were falling into an unproductive pattern of repetition and diagnosis, with little, if any, sense of empowerment or impulses toward change. Ellen said, "As I listened to Gary, I began to tell myself, 'There is more going on here than I am getting. What am I missing? I am framing these conversations like the VA therapists—"are you getting up, are you getting out, are you looking for a job that interests you?"—and like them seem to be gaining understanding and offering support but not seeing any directions of change.' I began to ask myself, 'What is missing here? What is there to learn that I am not seeing?'"

From the awareness of repetitious stuckness, Ellen said, "Suddenly I found a new thought emerging from within myself. I said to Gary, 'Gary, tell me more about the story of Afghanistan.' He did. He was full of tears talking about a buddy who was blown up and the children and families who were killed. He was focused on the loss, not the guilt. It was horrifying to him."

"As I listened, I found a new thought emerging in my mind, which was awareness of a new resource in Gary. I am not sure where it came from, but it would not leave. It kept growing. I said to him, 'Oh my God, Gary. For a person to feel as deeply about this as you do, must mean that you have a lot of compassion in the core of your soul.'"

Gary sat up. There was an energy shift in the room. "Really?"

Ellen: "Think about it."

Gary: "It is probably true. I have never thought of this."

Ellen: "Do you want to work on this? It is something to consider. You could work on living out of your compassion. That would be different than defining yourself by your depression and PTSD."

Gary: "Yes. That would be good."

Ellen: "Okay. Let's see where this goes. We will proceed slowly and find your way. You have been locked into thinking of yourself as a failure and defective because of horrible events in Afghanistan and haven't been able to get on with your life. But your feelings of horror come from your ability to have deep feelings of sadness and compassion. Compassion and sadness are really healthy responses to your situation. This can be the basis for seeing yourself in a different light. It will take some practice, but we can work on that together. It sounds like you want to give it a try."

Gary: "I do."

From this poignant exchange, a new dimension emerged in the counseling. Ellen said, "We are working on his identifying compassion and concern in himself and making that available in small steps in his life. It is slow but effective. He feels less depressed and reports some actions that make him feel good about himself. One thing we agreed on is that he will focus every day on identifying the compassionate parts of himself and acting on them at least once. Another example is his desire to let his story be told in your book. He feels that he can help others to face difficult things and find a way through them too."

As Ellen and I talked about what happened to shift the focus from repetitious naming of his depression and failed sense of self, we saw how she helped him name more directly at an emotional level the events in Afghanistan that were draining his soul. She moved from naming the effects to naming the precipitating events in an emotionally safe relationship.

The turning point for Ellen came when she tuned in to her own inner dialogue, as befits a collaborative conversation. There were two places where this occurred. First, she recognized that the discourse between her and Gary was becoming predictable and stagnant, leading nowhere. That prompted a different question about what actually happened in Afghanistan that touched his emotions and generated his belief that he was defective. Second, being alive to her inner dialogue evoked by his painful horror of the lives lost in Afghanistan led to reframing his identity as compassionate rather than defective. She, in effect, discovered in terms that felt true to the core of his being that his deep feelings about the welfare of his fellow human beings had not been lost in the traumatic events in war. The trauma both heightened and disguised his strong moral sensibilities about human welfare. Ellen's framing his pain as a mirror of compassion rather than a portrait of failure landed with force in his psyche. The energy level changed in the room. His negative self-judgment was reset. The core truth about his soul was that it was compassionate, not flawed. Ellen came to see this dimension of his life through open dialogue with him and with her own soul. She proffered it as a possibility for him to consider, rather than as a diagnosis or treatment goal. He immediately saw the deeper and more positive truth about himself. He and Ellen now had a revised basis for assisting him to enact his compassion in daily living. No longer is the focus of their work on Gary's depression, self-denigration, and job search but on living out of his compassion. Gary and Ellen are in an ongoing collaborative process of enacting a new set of behaviors and feelings, and of revising his core sense of self. Gary's moral compass has been reset. He had been heading south for a long time, and getting more and more lost. Now he has gained a view of his True North and with Ellen's collaboration is slowly but surely heading in a positive direction more true to himself.

Before concluding this strategic example, highlighting a couple of the features of collaborative conversation and reprocessing moral injury is in order. Ellen has developed a collaborative habit of mind and employs it astutely in her pastoral counseling. All of us can apply what she did in our own conversations, in spite of our contexts.

The first thing to recognize is how PTSD and moral injury are not easily separable in Gary's experience. Is he carrying PTSD from being a witness to violent death and destruction, or is he carrying moral injury with respect to his own actions? Certainly he is dealing with traumatic loss of friends and comrades in battle. Grieving these losses is a core matter for him, and one not addressed so far in my conversations with Ellen. He is also traumatized by witnessing the deaths of civilians, especially children. But, there is no evidence that he himself is struggling with a sense of moral injury resulting from his own actions. His negative self-judgment arises from a sense of defective agency concerning his ability to get his life going now. He is self-condemning because he cannot get his life in gear. He lost his marriage and a job he loved. In my judgment, these losses, and his sense of horror at the violent loss of life in Afghanistan, have led to an unrecognized moral injury. His moral injury is seen in the negative moral judgments he holds against himself, and not in actions he took against others. His moral compass—his sense of what gives value and significance to his life—dials him up as flawed. His life is wrong. He cannot get it right. "The good he would do, he does not." The trauma of war and the losses after war have conjoined to leave him with a moral injury expressed through self-condemnation as a defective soul who cannot make his life work in spite of genuine attempts to succeed. There is a fluid interplay between PTSD and moral injury in his case, and the VA and Ellen are aligned in helping him navigate these significant challenges.

The second thing to underscore is how Ellen's naming the various elements of Gary's life, beyond those dominant in his consciousness, is a co-creative process that joins and enhances the natural human resiliency necessary to bear and overcome traumatic challenges. Naming the full array of one's truth—prehending the total gestalt—emphasizes strength and renewal over impairment and failure. The key point here is that there is always more to the story that will provide a positive way to frame or reframe one's truth—if we persist in listening and speaking.

Third, as noted in the section above, curiosity is at the center of the caregiving conversations I am proposing. Curiosity is the vital medium for naming collaboratively the painful conundrums we face. Ellen demonstrated open-minded and appreciative curiosity. She says,

> I am always curious with people....I want to understand their lives and to hear pieces of their lives that they don't hear. I tell them what I hear in tentative, collaborative, and dialogical terms....I turn a mirror to the person so they can see their own goodness.

She discloses how sharing one's inner dialogue about what is interesting and exciting is the means of normalizing the abnormal and creating a new bond of care and safety between two people. Through curious interest and pursuit of salient new knowledge, fresh solutions come into view; contextually creative outcomes are discovered rather than applied. Ellen demonstrates the power of "prehending the total gestalt" by tuning into her deeper emotional self-talk arising from her conversations with Gary. When she reframed Gary's horror and self-abasement into compassion, there was a life-changing shift in the energy field between them.

Fourth, Ellen shows what can happen when we assist one another to emphasize our assets rather than our deficiencies. This is more than "positive or wishful" thinking; it is an affective connection to what is felt to be true at the deepest levels of our souls. Ellen puts it this way:

> Humans are seeking to know they are valued and lovable. I find that place where their humanness makes them genuinely lovable and valuable. Life and trauma take that away. Soul wounds jeopardize that sense of goodness and lovableness. I want to bring that forward. Finding Gary's compassionate self began to make that happen for Gary.

Ellen found her way to that lovable space in Gary through active listening and collaborative engagement. Once that core strength was discovered and affirmed, Gary could correct his misjudgments about himself and begin to build his life around the compassion he was learning to recognize in himself. This brings to mind David Chethlahe Paladin's spiritual discipline of "looking for the gift" in all people and circumstances.

Fifth, Ellen's conversation with Gary shows the need to join the emotional level and to identify meaningful action items that can be employed to change feelings and behaviors. There is more to collaborative healing than talk, cognitive framing, and immersion in feelings; there must meaningful actions based on one's felt strengths. Defective agency must be corrected by contextually creative practices. To make guilt and shame productive in one's life we must turn them into action items based on the individual's underlying but often hidden positive capacities to be a good person and do the right thing. We must help one another move from bodily emotions to bodily behaviors. Making this move will neutralize the isolation, paralysis, and self-condemnation that moral injury leaves inside us.

Sixth, in addition to naming, framing, and enacting, there must be a phase of revising one's self-assessment and moral actions in the light of these prior steps. It is too soon in the process to discern how Gary is revising his life based on compassion. The test of change will be based on his capacity to receive and integrate, or anchor, the positive outcomes of what he has been doing to live out of the positive sides of his soul. Without the capacity or power to receive new influences, there is no power to change or revise our lives. But we must remember that receiving something is very difficult, and takes moral courage too.[9]

Habits of Mind Exercise: Inner Dialogue on Healing Soul Wounds

This chapter is the heart of the book. It weaves into a usable whole the theological, psychological, and practical strategies to understand and respond to moral dissonance, dilemmas, and injury. What was your inner dialogue as you read through the chapter? Where did it touch you? What can you do with the insights you gleaned from your inner dialogue with the author? Where did you fight with this material? How would you improve upon it in your context? Specifically, how did the presentation of Gary's healing process impact your thinking? How can you make use of this in your own healing, or in your work with others? What other thoughts and strategies seem important for you to anchor? Where might you fashion practical adaptations to your own style and situations?

The examples used in this chapter centered on individuals, with background attention to communal, contextual, and ritual factors. We turn now to suggest how ritual practices and public memorials can be enormously significant in addressing moral injuries to individuals as well as to the body politic and sacred community.

For Further Reading

Brite Divinity School Soul Repair Center. www.brite.edu/programs/soul-repair/.

Moon, Zachary. *Coming Home Ministry That Matters with Veterans and Military Families*. St. Louis: Chalice, 2015.

Rambo, Shelly. *Resurrecting Wounds: Living in the Afterlife of Trauma*. Waco, TX: Baylor University Press, 2017.

CHAPTER 10
Healing Rituals and Memorials

This chapter explores the moral dimensions of communal ritual practices that help us bear and heal from the moral injuries brought on by corporate catastrophic disruptions. I especially address the healing of individuals and communities through rituals of lamentation in the context of public memorials.

Ritual practice is the universal human medium for community, meaning, and morality. Rituals bind us together and set us apart. They establish our world views and the mythologies by which we live and die. They set our moral compasses. Ritual practices sustain our efforts to reach our moral destinations. Rituals help us negotiate the moral dissonances and conflicts that we must address. Rituals guide our choices in moral dilemmas. And ritual practices sustain us in times of moral injury; they braid us into the healing powers of our communities. Indeed, they are the central means by which communities heal themselves when wounded by disaster and broken by moral failures.

Religious communities are particularly well-practiced when it comes to rituals. Rituals sacralize life cycle events from birth to death, and rituals are plentiful for addressing significant intrusive life challenges such as natural disasters, tragic loss, and various social and political disruptions. They are widely used for individual and communal healing, solidarity in challenging times, and spontaneous celebrations of unexpected providences.

Most of the rituals regularly practiced by religious communities can be readily employed to address moral injury. For Christians, the Eucharist is both a fellowship meal in which all "sorts and conditions" of participants are welcomed as morally flawed as well as communally important. The practice of confession of sins is a normalized practice in some churches by which moral failures are named, and then reframed in terms of forgiveness and reenacted in service and revising one's moral history.

Funerals and memorial services quickly lend themselves to honoring the moral impact of the deceased. When military honors are part of the service, it is easy to feel the esteem in which the departed is held for their service to their country. Obituaries and eulogies often recount the virtuous accomplishments of the loved one. Included are expressed or implied appeals to the community to follow their positive moral example.

Funeral and memorial services also offer a setting to release or forgive the deceased for harm they may have caused. Now that they are gone it becomes possible to reassess the relationship. Letting go of resentment will free us from the past. Foregoing expectations of future revenge or reconciliation will free the living to affirm the positive contributions of the deceased. Such a release can have powerful healing effects for soul wounds.

I am less familiar with ritual practices designed to bear on moral injury and moral healing in other than Christian traditions. Rabbi Harold Kushner wrote a Seder for American Jewish soldiers returning from war to assist with the moral challenges remaining after war and to facilitate a reentry to their civilian life.[1] The Soul Repair Center at Brite Divinity School developed an impressive interfaith liturgy, adapting elements from existing ritual practice in a variety of religious traditions, to assist individuals and communities to find acceptance and healing from the moral wounds of war.[2]

However, with respect to moral challenges, rituals are not only positive resources. They reflect and sometimes initiate moral dissonance, dilemmas, and even injury. In every ritual practice, as in every moral commitment, contending visions of the true and the good come into focus. On the positive side, rituals may suppress or channel virulent dissonance, protecting the community from inordinate harm and moral injury. They may even promote tolerance and respect for difference. On the negative side, ritual practices may be the source of brokenness and wounding. They may reinforce resentment and outrage by one community toward another.

For example, when All Saints' Day, Veterans Day, and Memorial Day rituals are performed to honor military service and those who died for their country, a series of questions about the morality of war and the relation of religion and nationality come to the fore. Many pastors have found it difficult to bridge the moral gaps in connection with these regular religious practices. A Protestant pastor I met at a conference in Germany recounted the great difficulty she encountered in a parish that devoted All Saints' Day to an extensive memorialization of those who lost their lives over the centuries in the various battles that took place between Germany and foreign invaders in that region. Significant conflict resulted from her futile attempts to broaden the theological interpretations of All Saints' Day and to bring other saints to the foreground. As we will explore, rituals and memorials carry a multidimensional valence that requires pastoral management if they are to be positive healing resources for moral injury resulting from our actions and the actions of others.

The pastoral caregiver, as a recognized moral authority and ritual leader, has a significant role to play when it comes to communal ritual practices in response to moral injury and moral healing. Understanding the dynamics of ritual practice and using them to ameliorate conflict, prevent injury, and heal from soul wounds is an indispensable element of the caregiver's role. Accordingly, I will profile some of the dimensions of healing moral injury in individuals and communities through public lamentation and memorializing losses.[3]

Corporate ritual practices are extremely important for individuals, such as soldiers, who otherwise must bear alone in the intricacies of their brains and psyches the costs of what the body politic as a whole has asked them to shoulder. Corporate ritual processes such as lamentation and memorialization also help the body politic itself to mourn its losses, share its anguish, confront its failings, honor or modify its values, and reinvest its hopes in a transformed future.

Lamentation, Memorials, and Healing

So, what is going on when we link rituals of lamentation and memorials in the public square? From the point of view of pastoral theology and care, personal and corporate cataclysms are not primarily something out there that we think about, but an inescapable course of history that we must live through. Our moral injuries are engendered by our direct and indirect immersion in the events of history, including natural disasters, war, and the dynamics of cultural hegemony. They are not simply past events. They are virulent ongoing diminishments. Moral injuries arising from war, for example, refashion our geographies and identities forever. We do not simply get over our entanglements in the world. We carry them, revise them, and live out of them. In the words of poet Edwin Muir, "war makes and remakes [us] ... still."[4] Lamentation joined with memorial events are positive human resources for making and remaking ourselves after (and sometimes during) war and other macrosystemic disruptions of our moral compasses.

When morally injurious disaster befalls us and lives are threatened or lost, two things occur at once: there is an instantaneous shattering of the world and there is an instantaneous survival reflex that responds to the shattering. The world that is coming apart is also a world that responds to hold itself together. We humans must find life-giving means of coping with existential threat and traumatic loss if we are to survive and thrive as individuals and communities.

Cataclysmic experiences, whether from natural disaster, sexual and domestic violence, or moral injury and PTSD from war, initiate a new history for the victims and the community. A trauma history is comprised of three sequential processes, that also feedback on one another. First there is shattering of one's world and soul. Second is the emergence of survival mechanisms. Third is the press for recovery and rebuilding. Religious communities and their leaders are intimately inscribed into the shattering, survival, and recovery plots of the trauma and moral injury narrative. Lamentation and memorializing are among our greatest contributions to the healing narratives we attempt to create from our wounding. Lamentation and memorializing address the initial shattering by the way they help us share our anguish together. They assist with survival needs by mobilizing resources to provide strength and refuge. They guide the recovery process through assessing causes, protesting injustices, sharing memories, reclaiming lost values, and reinvesting hope.

Pastoral theologian Kathleen Billman, theologian Daniel L. Migliore, and biblical scholar Kathleen O'Connor help us to understand lamentation as a strength-inducing religious resource. It is by no means simply "wallowing in pain" and "being stuck in weakness." The central purpose of lamentation is to provide a way for individuals and communities to truthfully express the sorrows of the world that have come upon them and to register protest, complaint, and anger at those responsible for them. As we fully name the truth of our affliction, paradoxically, that affliction becomes bearable and the way is opened toward healing.[5] According to O'Connor, when we reflect back the suffering we hear from one another "it restores the humanity of the victim because it validates their perception of the way the world has fallen away from their feet."[6] Billman and Migliore argue that lamentation helps us to acknowledge the truthful reality of our pain and to reconnect with the innate goodness of our personal and corporate lives by

> offering a needed language of pain; confirming the value of embodied life; granting permission to grieve and protest; challenging inadequate understandings of God and preparing the way for new understandings; strengthening our self-understanding as responsible agents; purifying anger and the desire for vengeance; increasing solidarity with others who suffer; and revitalizing praise and hope.[7]

Lamentation is a mode of recapturing strength and moving toward healing and morally energized engagement with our wounding world. It moves beyond personal grief and demise to embrace and be embraced by vital community energies by which we may sustain, guide, and heal one another and our broken world. The religious leader and pastoral caregiver can assist personal and communal healing by working with others in the community, including the secular milieu, to develop lamentation rituals and a variety of memorials that heal and guide the community.

Billman, Migliore, and O'Connor show us that lamentation is more than holding one another together in the face of our pain and grief. I have identified three interacting poles of lamentation: sharing anguish, interrogating causes, and reinvesting hope. These are to be considered as circular and spiraling rather than linear and sequential. I find that this tripartite framework provides a helpful way for naming, reframing, enacting, and revising our moral values and organizing world views in the light of what we face as communities and individuals when our worlds are shattered. They also help us address our own complicity and responsibility for participation in actions and structures of life that harm others. Lamentation rituals usually take place in the context of public memorials, which gives them both significance in the here and now and set the stage for the long-term recovery process.

Sharing Anguish

Sharing anguish in public contexts serves the survival as well as the recovery plot. The instant our lives are shattered by traumatic cataclysms we are gripped by shock, confusion, disbelief, fear, and anguish. We spontaneously band together to support one another and to rescue and protect others. The role of religious communities and leaders becomes critical at this point. By offering refuge and providing rituals to articulate loss and to support efforts to stabilize and respond, the pastoral leader and religious bodies help us bear the unspeakable anguish that now binds us together.[8]

At the onset of disaster, an incredible unity and solidarity come into place. While the membranes are ruptured, the connective ligaments are tightened and perhaps for the first time a society feels like an acutely bonded community. There is massive togetherness, but there is also an intense individualization that we each feel when our lives are in peril and something threatening has come upon us.

In this context of initial sharing of anguish, spontaneous shrines creatively pop up. For example, at Columbine High School in Littleton, Colorado, someone erected fifteen crosses in a local park for all those who died. Others brought flowers and mementos. Lawn signs, license plates, buttons, and public billboards all carried the message, "We are Columbine!" In these violent traumas, healing from moral injury begins when the community bonds together to memorialize the dead, celebrate their lives, and affirm one another in the face of terror and violence. It is a time to begin to name what was lost, to honor the dead, and to begin to construct a narrative of events to frame how the community will remember what happened and articulate its meaning.

Strategic Example:
A Muslim Lament

As an example of the vital role played by ritual in support of individual and communal moral healing, I would like to share a portion of a family interview I did in Bosnia and Herzegovina. This interview took place as a part of my research on the impact of war on the pastoral care of families. This vignette has helped me shape the discussion of lament and memorials and go deeper into their interconnections in relation to moral injury and soul repair at individual, familial, and corporate levels.

Mrs. B. and her twenty-five-year-old daughter, Amina, described how an annual memorial service helped them to name their anguish before God and one another and to protest the injustice of what happened.[9] Mrs. B. reported that on the evening of May 25, 1995, her seventeen-year-old niece, Lejla, went to the town square in Tuzla with her best friend Sonia to hang out with other young people. Rockets were fired into the square a little after 8 p.m. Seventy-one people were killed and two hundred more were injured. Since Tuzla was populated by Serbs and Croats as well as Muslims, all three groups were affected.

Mrs. B. and Amina were very worried about Lejla. Mrs. B. and her husband joined Lejla's parents to look for her. They finally discovered that she and Sonia had been killed. The shock and grief were overwhelming. Mrs. B. agonizingly asked, "Why should someone do this to other humans? Only God can take life. Why is this happening to us?" Her piercing lament was echoed by others in her family. Amina said that she saw her uncle's face at a televised funeral service. "I will never forget how he looked! When I saw his face I realized that this is not a nightmare that I will wake up from, but that my cousin is really gone. Try to imagine somebody who has always been a happy person suddenly crushed, pale face, and I could see that he lost his heart, soul, and his life. My uncle and aunt started to smile again just a few years ago, but never like before they lost their daughter. But at that moment when I saw him on TV I knew that Lejla was gone and that our lives would never be the same."

Mrs. B. and Amina told how this affected their family. They are still in great pain about the attack. The anguish that they expressed was intense and unfiltered; it was very distressing to the translator and to me to experience directly the level of hurt that they demonstrated in telling the story. Mrs. B. carries in her purse a poem that was written for a memorial service to lament and protest these deaths on the first anniversary of the attack. She finds great comfort in it. She read the poem out loud in our interview. Her daughter later sent me a translation.

The poem of lament by Nijaz Alispahic is read at a memorial service held each year in Tuzla. It is called "Overcoming Pain." It is a lament that links the community's ongoing pain of loss with the longing for vindication and accountability. (The phrases "Mother raised Sulejman" and "Golden sun, say hello to my old mother" are titles of old Bosnian folk songs and poetry.)

Overcoming Pain

That night they did not shoot at the city
They shot at "Mother raised Sulejman"
At "Golden sun, say hello to my old mother"
They shot at our soul,
At the poem,
At silver moon light,
They shot at the narrow eyebrow of a girl,
At the iris of our eyes they shot,
They shot at our prayers,
Killed those who were sleepy and in love,
Killed the desire of two coasts to come together,
That night Tuzla's Kapija [Center City] was the birth place of:
Sorrow among sorrows,
Grudge among grudges,
Poem among poems.
They extinguished the light in pearl lakes.
Dear God!
Let them be punished,
those who brought us this pain,
which we will never overcome[10]

This lament takes place at a memorial site.[11] The community draws together in solidarity and compassion. The ritual of lament at this site enables the community to feel and to bear together the pervasive sense of loss and the anguish that remains from the tragedy of violent aggression at the hand of former countrymen. It is a vehicle for naming those who are responsible, protesting the injustice, and calling for accountability. Rather than leaving persons and communities broken and isolated, public lamentation in the memorial context allows new questions to be asked, new answers formulated, and new histories to be imagined and named.[12]

Chapter 10

Interrogating Causes

As I faced the horror of Hurricane Katrina and the violence at Columbine; 9/11; Newtown, Connecticut; Charleston, South Carolina; and so many other places where life was destroyed under such cruel circumstances, I found many questions seeping into mind. What happened? Who did it? Why did this happen? Is the universe a moral place? Did God cause this? Why did God not prevent it?

These questions are a part of the healing properties of lamentation. Lamentation provides more than a place to cry. As seen in Mrs. B.'s lament and the poem read at the Tuzla memorial, lamentation also gives us the place to question, complain, protest, and assess responsibility for what happened. By questioning, we devise ways to name and frame what happened so that we might bear the costs and heal from the consequences of the wounds to our souls and communities. Our questions become more hostile and accusatory and demand clear answers when the tragedy is at the hand of fellow human beings. They lead to moral judgments, and sometimes to moral condemnation of the actors. Interrogating causes and focusing complaints at undeserved disaster adds theological strength and moral dimensionality to the lamentation and memorializing process. Lamentation in the context of memorialization discloses that we are creatures of culturally constructed histories and meanings; we are not determined by fate!

Mrs. B. asked through tears and shrieks, "Why should someone do this to other humans? Only God can take life. Why is this happening to us?" The question of moral responsibility comes to the foreground in public lamentation and memorials, and the question of God is always connected to what happened. As we have seen in chapters 5 and 8, one of the central questions for monotheistic faith is God's relation to the situation. Is God responsible? If so, "O God, hear my complaint against you for this adversity." If not, "Where is God? Is God's power too feeble to prevent and offset the powers of evil and destruction that disaster brings upon us? Or does God have divine intentions in mind?" Religious communities and their leaders are expected to engage the many forms that these theological questions take, or to at least acknowledge the integrity of those sincerely asking for guidance about God's role in the dissolution of God's world. Mrs. B. answered this question for herself by asserting that it was not God who took those lives in Tuzla. They were taken by fellow humans who should be punished for doing what only God has a right to do. Another form of the questions of God's involvement in death and destruction arises in wartime when some soldiers ask why they were spared while other soldiers, who they deemed to be better human beings, were not spared. (Survivor's guilt now comes into play as a moral issue for those spared.)

I have wrestled hard personally and professionally with the question of God's moral responsibility for tragic disasters in history. It is from the standpoint of what is actually experienced in the middle of disaster that I have found ways of constructively responding to the interrogating questions about God that disaster inevitably evokes. It is from *within* tragedy and trauma—not outside or above—that the questions of God's goodness and power have clarified for me.

As we have already seen, at the very moment when disaster crashes into us there is also engendered an acute life-giving sense of being bonded together with one another to protect and preserve life. This compassionate bonding is the power of life responding to death. This compassionate bonding is the power of love in the face of violence; it is the energy of hope combating hopeless circumstances. It is contextual creativity seeking direction for a viable repair of the fractured world that has come upon us.

Many survivors of catastrophe and their first responders and caregivers report that this intense harmony and compassionate service were life-changing for them. They felt that they were more themselves and more vitally connected to one another and to the most important values of their lives than ever before. Indeed, the 9/11 Memorial and Museum combines recognition of absence while articulating renewed commitment to the life-affirming power of dedicated and sacrificial service given to one another at the very point in time when life was being brutally extinguished before our very eyes. Some persons say that they have never felt the presence and power of God more clearly than when responding to the extreme needs of disaster victims and recovering the bodies lost in the rubble.[13]

How then can it be, theologically speaking, that the same event that horrifies and disgusts us is simultaneously embraced as an occasion of renewing what is most valued and important to us? How does a life-destroying event become a life-giving event for those surviving it? It is here that we find the keystone for thinking of God's relation to the catastrophic moment.

One theological response is to affirm that the God who is in control of the universe orchestrated or permitted these horrendous circumstances for the very purpose of engendering the positive values of compassion, community, and hope that they make possible. A good and all-powerful God bends everything to God's purposes. The spiritual call, then, is to affirm the strong connections that sustain us while incorporating the losses into the greater spiritual advance that the losses make possible in the immediate and long term. He or she who has lost much, loves more and hopes more joyfully. True, the losses may be great, but they serve the greater good of soul-making and community building. In the words of St. James, then, when trials come upon us, we can count it as all good for the testing of our faith because the result of trials is steadfastness.[14] I believe that this is the default view of God's relation to suffering, catastrophe, and loss in monotheistic traditions.

Chapter 10

A second theological response is to recognize that when disaster comes upon us, it has arisen from multiple interacting processes of history, culture, and nature rather than from intentional or passive acts of God. Disaster instantly changes our history. It initiates a new history in the very instant it stomps into time and space. If one believes that God is the power of life in opposition to all the powers of sin, evil, and death—rather than an agent of tragedy and loss—then it follows that the very instant of cataclysm is also the very instant of the divine response in human history. The interweaving of human solidarity, service, and protection universally experienced in the moment of catastrophe is made possible by God's strategic response to the destructive elements in the universe. God's bonding power in the face of tragic catastrophe is not a new form of divine compassion and power, but another upsurge of God's sustaining and transforming goodness within the messy unfolding of the universe and the vulnerability of human life.

I find the second theological option more promising. It lets God off the hook for the onset of destructiveness and evil. It avoids the tortured conundrum of trying to wrest a positive divine purpose out of despicably evil and undeserved circumstances. Rather, it finds in God the basis for the efficacious presence of grace, power, and caring human community in response to the tragedies that both throw us into the abyss and bring us together at the same time. God is our ally. God is our co-creative partner in healing, sustaining, and guiding the shaken, shattered, exploded, bombed, bulleted, and drowning human community. It is God who stands behind and makes moral sense of Mrs. B.'s anguished cry for accountability, punishment, and vindication. God is the moral center of the universe and is the basis for our hope that something positive might come into place in spite of our devastations and moral failures.

If God is construed as an empowering ally in this process, rather than an ambivalent or ambiguous murky force obscured by, but somehow responsible for, cataclysmic events, we are better able to inquire into what natural and human circumstances have led to these disasters. We are free to probe into the causes and hold accountable the elemental human and natural forces that have come together to create monstrous circumstances. Assuming human and natural causes, rather than divine agency, allows us to protest, complain, contend and wrest power from those forces that damage us and diminish the world. Lamentation and the memorializing process give the structure for us to contend with one another about the meanings and responsibility for evil and to fashion new approaches to living from what we discover. They are sites where we can express our anguish, voice our complaints, and protest the injustice of what has come upon us. For example, many (but not all) veterans of combat come to ask themselves questions about why they chose to act against their core values by taking lives in war—sometimes with pride, and even pleasure. Discerning these motivations and consequences is part of what addressing moral injury is about for veterans. Many veterans who are struggling with questions about killing in war and might find that the "interrogating causes" dimensions of lamentation and memorialization will help them come to terms with what is and is not theirs to bear.[15] In any case, discerning the various levels of accountability for both individuals and social groups is a step toward healing, memory, and repair.[16]

Strategic Example: Interrogating Causes at the Vietnam Wall

The Vietnam Veterans Memorial in Washington, DC, is a memorial that seeks to promote healing from the losses and moral injuries of war. It provides a setting for lamentation: a place to share anguish, interrogate causes, and reinvest hope. The "Wall," as it is referred to, was originally designed to begin a healing process. "Healing meant many things to many people. . . . Could it heal the chasm within society, promote closure, show gratitude for those who served, comfort those in grief and remind future generations of the toll wrought by war?"[17] A major concern was whether it could accomplish all of this without reawakening all of the contending political and cultural dissonance that continues to wound our society. We had become morally divided as a nation about Vietnam; that moral injury continues in the psyches of individuals and families who both supported and opposed the war, and continues to infuse our contemporary consciousness about military options today.

The Wall has become a site for active engagement in memorializing lamentation and recovering from war. The Wall's caretaker's calls what happens there "Wall Magic."[18] Wall Magic refers to coincidental events that bring people together in surprising and healing ways. Strangers meet for the first time in front of the name of someone they cherished and share memories and stories about the fallen veteran. Students on field trips learn about the history of their country, and about what it means to share the anguish of war. When asked by her teacher to leave something at the Wall that represents an irrevocable loss for them, one student left the only picture she had of her veteran father taken before he was killed in Vietnam.[19]

Memorial sites such as the Wall help us keep our histories above-ground and before us. When our histories are above-ground, in our grasp, we can name them and make them our own. And we can fashion something healing and hopeful through reframing and reenacting them. By sharing the anguish of our histories together and working hard to understand their impacts upon us, we are better able to bear and revise them together.

But the Wall is not only a healing site. It is a site of contending values, disputed narratives, and conflicting histories. It is a site of interrogation, discordant memories, and dissonant implications for how life is to be reclaimed and hope reinvested.

Dueling mythic histories have arisen from the Wall. One example centers on a disputed account of what actually happened and who was responsible for the napalm bombing of the South Vietnam village of Trang Bang on July 8, 1972. Many of us remember the iconic picture of the young semi-clad girl burning with napalm running down a road. It was a sensory experience of war that cemented many Americans against the mythic justifications for our involvement in Vietnam.

One orienting narrative that has arisen at the Wall is about how the young girl in the picture, Kim Phuc, survived her wounds, healed, and, in a dramatic ceremony at the Wall during Veterans Day weekend in 1996, forgave the American pilot who bombed her village and injured her.[20] John Plummer, a former Army Captain, who by this time had become a Methodist minister, was in attendance at the ceremony. At an appropriate point, he came forth and indicated that he was that pilot. She offered forgiveness. Their interaction was expanded into a documentary and became the dominant narrative about sharing anguish, accepting responsibility, and moving forward through forgiveness. This history has continued to be told, in various forms, as an inspiring example of healing and new life. For Plummer and Kim, memorializing lamentation about specific acts in war afforded a public setting to move beyond personal and private anguish, and to reengage their public histories—to externalize what they had carried—and to have their histories validated in time and place. It also gave them a chance to move beyond the frozen past to revise their moral histories and to discover new opportunities for human understanding and healing. By accepting our responsibilities for injury, we are able to find constructive ways to live.

There is, however, a contending narrative about what happened in Vietnam that day in 1972 and who was responsible for it.[21] According to this narrative, the bombing was not by Americans. No Americans were in the village or vicinity, and the village was not a target for bombing. The pilot who dropped the bombs was a pilot in the South Vietnamese Air Force. The battle was near the village, not in it. The four canisters of napalm were dropped accidentally. Captain Plummer, in fact, had no role in what happened; he was not the pilot of the plane and did not order the attacks as he claimed.[22] To say that an American was responsible for what happened is viewed by some as a fraudulent use of history. Ronald Timberlake contends that the link of the bombing to Americans was made for the first time by Jan Scruggs, the founder and president of the Vietnam Veterans Memorial Fund, at the beginning of the ceremony in 1996 at which Kim Phuc spoke and Rev. Plummer appeared. According to Timberlake, before this orchestration of the memorial ceremony, there was never a claim that Americans had a part in the bombing; the narrative history was fabricated to serve other purposes. Timberlake's narrative interrogates the assessment of causes and responsibility for the bombing of Trang Bang and Kim Phuc's injuries. Those holding to this second narrative argue that Kim Phuc's forgiveness would be better directed to her countrymen and the pilot of her country's Air Force than to Captain

Plummer and the Americans. Otherwise, unnecessary shame and blame compound rather than ameliorate the complex levels of moral injury that we still carry from the Vietnam War.

From the dissonance between these views, we see that lamentation and memorial sites bring various parties and perspectives together (though not always in an ameliorative way). Memorializing lamentation and interrogating causes in the context of moral injury is not an easy or unambiguous matter. The discord that inevitably emerges can result in increased anguish, contentious interrogation, and insurmountable obstacles to rebuilding a common future. Yet it is important to have these public venues to contain, name, reframe, enact, and revisit our moral histories. To move on, there need to be sites where the events and parties can engage our moral histories publicly and wrestle with discordant assessments. While agreement about historical events may elude our grasp, having a public context to identify and engage our multiple narratives can assist us in understanding and even normalizing our dissonance, and fashioning our disparate hopes toward future possibilities. Public memorials endure over time and anchor our moral injuries in concrete places. They become an ongoing resource to honestly name the diversity and dissonance we are living through, and to creatively reframe, reenact, and revisit our moral injuries as a part of our healing.[23]

Reinvesting Hopes

In addition to providing a context for sharing anguish, honoring the dead, constructing memory, and interrogating causes, lamentation in the context of memorialization enables us to reclaim life and to reinvest in the future. The structure of lament in connection with memorial practice usually reaffirms the core virtues of the community and commits to bringing them to bear to change the world.

The 9/11 Memorial and Museum, for example, names the anguish, assigns responsibility for the catastrophe, and recommits to a hopeful future. Their website explains,

> The Museum honors the nearly 3,000 victims of these attacks and all those who risked their lives to save others. It further recognizes the thousands who survived and all who demonstrated extraordinary compassion in the aftermath. Demonstrating the consequences of terrorism on individual lives and its impact on communities at the local, national, and international levels, the Museum attests to the triumph of human dignity over human depravity and affirms an unwavering commitment to the fundamental value of human life.[24]

Lamentation is not a process of wallowing in pain, loss, and victimhood. It is a way of carrying the past with strength and funding the future with hope. By naming the costs of disaster, sharing its pain in public venues, and interrogating its causes, the human community is drawn together to work for our highest values. Reinvesting hope involves moving from the discernment of causes to accepting responsibility, changing behaviors, and building new patterns of community. Change may be required at the personal and interpersonal levels, as well as on a macrosystemic level such as rearranging economic, political, cultural, and religious meaning-systems and practices. Memorials inscribe these values in history, give them a place to stand, and provide direction for investing our hopes that they will be more fully realized over time. In terms of healing from moral injuries, the meanings and understandings mediated through public memorials and lamentation assist us in the naming, reframing, reenacting, and revising our moral histories in contextually creative and communally significant ways.

Strategic Example: Reinvesting Hopes at Sand Creek

I would like to briefly highlight some recent efforts in Colorado to address an ongoing moral injury that binds us together in our state. The state of Colorado has worked hard to understand and lament more fully our harmful actions toward Native Americans over the centuries. The year 2014 marked the 150-year anniversary of the Sand Creek massacre, in which nearly seven hundred American troops led by a prominent United Methodist Minister, Col. John Chivington, massacred up to 133 peaceful Indians, over a hundred of which were women and children. In December 2014, Governor John Hickenlooper of Colorado apologized to the descendants of the massacre, stating that "we will not run from this history."[25]

In addition, the Rocky Mountain Conference of the United Methodist Church devoted its 2014 Annual Conference to "Healing Relationships with Native Peoples." As a part of this commitment, the Conference worked carefully with Native Americans to structure a conference-wide journey to the Sand Creek Massacre National Memorial Site.[26] At the same time, the University of Denver, a United Methodist-related school, was celebrating its 150-year anniversary. As a part of its commemoration, the University of Denver also assessed their implication in the Sand Creek massacre. A statement from its website says, "The massacre occurred when John Evans, founder of the University of Denver and of Northwestern University in Illinois, was serving both as governor of the Colorado Territory and as territorial superintendent of Indian affairs."[27]

In her inauguration as the University's eighteenth (and first female) chancellor, Rebecca Chopp stated,

> Our democratic ideals make our unique and diverse system of higher education the engine for the future of our society.... But let us also tell the truth: Our nation and our institutions of higher education often fall short of our aspirations. Unfortunately, we share tragic histories of injustice, including the denial of freedoms and the intrinsic and legal rights of Native American peoples, specifically with respect to the Arapahoe and Cheyenne tribes who once lived and thrived on this very land. The events of Sand Creek, and the suffering experienced there, bear stark witness to injustice, injustice that we now aspire to make right. Even as such events from our past remind us of our failures, our renewed ideals and aspirations provoke us to strive for justice and fuel our impatience to do even better for all people.[28]

Chancellor Chopp, a Methodist minister and Christian theologian, made her installation a memorial and lamentation of past offences, sharing anguish, accepting responsibility, and pledging to invest hopes in a new, yet unfinished, future. Her call to this ongoing commitment to making a new history with Native Americans was made good in part by her invitation to Tink Tinker, a Native American activist on the faculty of the Iliff School of Theology (a close affiliate of DU), to bless her installation with a feather-wand ritual for her and a benediction to the gathered community.

I asked Tinker for his reflection on these various attempts to revisit our bloody and rapacious histories centering on Sand Creek. He pointed me to a video clip of his address to the General Conference of the United Methodist Church in 2012.[29] In this clip, he made four points relative to healing moral injuries. First, he said we are all related as humans, and all reality—rivers, animals, rocks, skies, water—are part of the totality of our lives. We are in this together and we must heal our lives and our relation to our world that we have all failed to some degree. Second, healing means repentance, which means concrete steps toward changing our ways. Third, he said that repentance and change are communal processes—not only individual—and are ongoing as we learn to see our histories more clearly and our opportunities more fully. Fourth, he said that it is critically important that the Euro-American dominant culture do its own hard work—and only those of us who are members of this particular culture can do this work—to understand our history with Native Americans in fuller detail and to take ownership of it. Tinker was clear that though we are all in this together, we are not all in it the same way. All parties must discern (i.e., interrogate) their particular contributions and take responsibility for repairing and changing what they have brought about.

Tinker and Chopp remind us that memorializing lamentation is hard, dangerous, and never-completed work. Sharing the anguish of remorse for wrongdoing and the pain resulting from our actions and the actions of our social groups, exploring the causes of our moral failures, and reinvesting in hope through repentance and rebuilding new lives together is ongoing. But through education, ritualization, respectful engagement, and honest accountability we can expect to find a way to something worthwhile in spite of our horrendous moral failures. It is through these memorial and lamentation processes that we are able to experience that "I am as we are," and to name our complicity in harming others. From this solidarity we can better frame the actions we need to take separately and together to continue our healing. By enacting new behaviors of care and justice-making, we can revisit our moral history and reinvest our hopes in finding true healing from the historical and cultural injuries that continue to wound our individual souls and our bodies politic.

Some Pastoral Considerations about Perilous Discourse

There are two dissonant features of public memorials. First, they are sites of engagement in which anguish, responsibility, forgiveness, and new hope can be mediated through a sense of communal togetherness and solidarity. Second, they are contested sites where the questions of causes, accountabilities, and what is necessary for positive outcomes can be fraught with danger and cause further harm. Lamentation and public remembrances are both comforting and dangerous.

Religious leaders providing personal and communal guidance to increase healing of moral injury must be particularly attentive to the contentious and often vitriolic dimensions of public lamentation. I think of some of the pastors who lost their jobs for preaching forgiveness for the shooters to their outraged congregations shortly after the Columbine shootings. I think of the harmful discourse around the proposal for a Muslim community center near the 9/11 Museum and Memorial. I think of the Protestant pastor who was reprimanded by his church for participating in the public memorial and lamentation service following the school shooting in Newtown, Connecticut. Memorial processes can incite rage and violence, especially when there is insufficient accountability by the offending agents and harm, rather than healing and understanding, continues to be perpetrated. My colleague Carrie Doehring has noticed that sometimes memorial processes, in the context of lamenting loss of life and community brokenness, can lead to an increase of fear and neglect of the welfare of others.[30] Further, it must be recognized that the pain of many traumatized individuals and communities may be deeper than words and rituals can express, leaving them irrevocably cut off from the healing discourse and practices of their communities.

Perhaps the most difficult lesson for those of us in dominant power positions is to recognize the truths of our own histories and the ongoing implications of the injuries our way of life has caused other parties. There is a tendency for dominant cultures to define the scope of permissible anguish, to have ultimate control over the discourse about causes, and to determine when it is time to get over the past and move on.

The lamentation and memorial process is not a three-step process that is finished and done with. It is a repetitive engagement over time—maybe centuries—to learn what happened and how things might truly be made right by the mutual efforts of all affected parties through time. And even then, it is essential to take our cues from the most vulnerable in the conversation.

To summarize and conclude, pastoral theologians and caregivers, along with our religious and secular communities, are compelled by corporate catastrophe to become immersed in efforts toward rescue, relief, and recovery. Along with the total community we become immediately inducted into God-inspired and life-ensuring efforts toward human survival and flourishing when trauma befalls us. In addition to the spontaneous upsurges of grace, power, and caring community that come into being the instant disruption occurs, we also have available to us a variety of cultural products that have arisen over the centuries to help human communities endure and transform the evils befalling or caused by us. Religious thought and ritual practice are central elements in this repertoire of human coping and healing. Lamentation in the context of public memorials offers immediate and long-term resources for survival and healing wounded individuals and communities. Religious and other communal sites become safe refuges for the displaced, injured, and dead when the storms of life are carrying everything away. Religious and other corporate rituals organize meaning, give voice to anguish, and call forth the moral values that sustain community and focus its responses over the long haul. Religious symbols and religious teachings, along with secular values and conventions, anchor the heart and mind within the enduring values of courage, sacrifice, and collective efforts for the greater good. All of this comes together in the processes of lamentation, mediated by a range of memorial options, where anguish is named, comfort shared, victims honored, memories constructed, questions asked, conflict focused, forgiveness mediated, and hopes invested in writing a morally viable story of a future worth having.

Habits of Mind Exercise

What was interesting and exciting to you as you read about the rituals of lamentation and memorialization? What challenged you? How might you modify them for your situation? What do they suggest for ways to adapt the rituals you already use in your ministry (and personal spirituality) to address moral dissonance and heal moral injury? How might your pastoral role be expanded and linked to public leadership in times of community conflict and crisis? What core values will guide your participation in morally conflicted public discourse? How do the resources from this book inform how you might become collaboratively engaged in a local moral challenge? I invite you to devise a strategic plan to enter this moral challenge and to involve your religious community as much as possible. What other responses come to mind? How will you act on them?

For Further Reading

Anderson, Herbert. "Violent Death, Public Tragedy, and Rituals of Lament: An Interfaith Agenda." *Ordo: Bath, Word, Prayer, Table: A Liturgical Primer in Honor of Gordon W. Lathrop.* Edited by Dirk G. Lange and Dwight W. Vogel, 188–200. Akron, OH: OSL Publications, 2005.

Arel, Stephanie N., and Shelly Rambo. *Post-Traumatic Public Theology.* Cham, Switzerland: Palgrave Macmillan, 2016.

Brock, Rita Nakashima. "Moral Conscience, Moral Injury, and Rituals for Recovery." In *Moral Injury and Beyond,* ed. Renos Papadopolous. Oxford: Taylor and Francis, 2017.

Solnit, Rebecca. "The Monument Wars." *Harper's,* January 2017. http://harpers.org/archive/2017/01/the-monument-wars/.

Tick, Edward. *War and the Soul: Healing Our Nation's Veterans from Post-Traumatic Stress Disorder.* Wheaton, IL: Quest Books, 2005. Tick provides a fuller discussion of rituals and resources for healing veteran PTSD.

Conclusion

I would like to employ the collaborative mindset to conclude this book, specifically to register the knowledge that has evolved or clarified from the efforts to produce this book. I will briefly address three questions: What do I know better now than I did before? What do I know now that I did not know before this sustained engagement with moral dissonance, dilemmas, and healing souls wounded by moral injury? What challenges and questions remain on which to base future conversations?

Confirmations: What I Know Better Now

At the end of this project, I am more confident that honest and trusting conversations are intrinsically valuable in addressing the unending moral conflicts we all face and the soul wounds we all carry. And while in some cases the collaborative frame is difficult to establish and maintain, it is a positive alternative to the diagnostic-treatment paradigm that dominants our professional and ordinary discourse. Naming, framing, enacting, and revising are usable constructs for collaborative and self-directed moral engagement and healing. They are trustworthy mechanisms through which contextual creativity reliably serves up life-altering options.

I knew before this project that there are always two sides to a story. But having completed the project I have become more deeply aware that good people make life-and-death commitments that can easily create moral enmity with other good people. I am much more aware at how intractable these differences can be, and how they can easily become sources of moral injury for individuals and communities. The best that collaborative conversations may be able to do in these polarizations is to contain unnecessary hostility and build protections against harm. Though I see more clearly the difficulty of fashioning a viable co-humanity across cultural, personal, and moral

– 153 –

differences, I remain convinced that we can never stop attempting to recognize the humanity of those whose moral actions we relentlessly oppose—and we can never stop insisting that they recognize ours. The moral tapestry of history is still being woven. Our contextually creative contributions are an integral part of what that tapestry will become.

The writing of this volume confirmed that moral engagement and moral healing are always social processes and not reducible to individual psychologies and motivational systems. The various levels of meaning of the aphorism "I am as we are" has taken on heightened significance in light of the concepts and practices employed in this book. I have also come to a deeper appreciation of the contributions of ritual, education, and lived practices in setting (and resetting) one's moral compass and healing moral injuries. Social and cultural embodiment is the territory of the soul: of its injury, its healing, and its vital efforts to do the right thing "in all our relations."

Finally, I have come to a clearer sense that alongside the intersectionality of oppression there is also the intersectionality of goodness. Ellen's counseling with Gary disclosed that this morally injured Afghanistan veteran's pain was connected to unrecognized compassion in his soul. His pain was motivated by something good in him that was not entirely captured by his witness to evil. Collaborative conversation takes us to many positive intersections in our souls and communities. Rituals link us with the vitality of healing and moral affirmation, as well as to the places of failure and challenge. Such recognition invites a resetting of our moral compasses so that we might better travel, and understand more fully, the many roads intersecting our moral lives.

Discoveries:
What I Did Not Know Before

A first surprise was to discover that it is a matter of survival for individuals and groups to possess intact moral compasses and have available effective healing methods for moral injury. I had always thought of moral integrity and health to be directed toward human thriving. Through this work, I see that they are more comprehensive than that. They are motivated by survival dynamics as well as the desire to flourish. The survival and well-being of the microsystem, mesosystem, and macrosystem—and the relationships between them—are fully dependent on the moral orientations and practices cultivated. Some moral values are lethal even though those holding them are motivated by what they believe is necessary for their survival and well-being. Human survival as well as individual fulfillment is at stake in how we set and follow our moral compasses and mediate moral healing.

Second, one of the most surprising discoveries is the awareness of where most moral living and moral healing take place: in rituals and routine social gatherings. Church picnics, friendships, interest groups, informal conversations, work-space engagements, ordinary and special rituals, and the active imaginations of persons and groups make doing right and being good more likely. As a theological educator and pastoral psychotherapist, I was especially surprised to learn that rituals do more for setting and correcting moral compasses than teaching beliefs and concepts. Practices carry more power than information and guidance. Collaborative conversation is a form of ritualized practice that shapes moral narratives and mediates moral healing.

Third, I always believed that love and relational justice were at the heart of Christian moral thought and practice, but I did not fully realize how difficult it is to meaningfully connect them to the moral challenges and victories that we actually face day-to-day. Most often we make decisions and then (sometimes) attach a theological label (such as love, forgiveness, justice, or reconciliation) to them. That label is often pretty generic, and may or may not reflect the actual energies within the soul and experience of the actor giving rise to the label. It seems promising to me in a way I had not seen before to create a kind of practical theological interpretation of religious themes by pressing more closely on the understandings arising from the collaborative healing process itself. Again, Ellen's work with Gary is suggestive of the way redeeming a wounded soul begins by reframing the pain as a mirror of compassion rather than an indicator of demise. The theological consequence of this experience might lead, for example, to understanding the religious theme of redemption becoming possible as a result of extracting the pain of compassion from the pain of the wounded soul. Such a move might strengthen our efforts to bring our concepts and our spiritual vitalities into closer alliance.

Challenges:
Curious and Difficult Questions

At the end of the day, I am also left with some very challenging questions: Can collaborative processes provide an alternative to the dominant contentious ethos of moral engagement in the mesosystem and macrosystem of church and culture? Can religious communities provide an alternative to the polarizing and morally injurious discourse that circumscribes much of our contemporary cultural mindset?

I am particularly eager to consider the questions: What potentials exist for collaborative conversation to make Internet-based discourse generative rather than polarizing? Can collaborative engagement move us beyond our siloed moral narratives?

In a communication milieu that is fast becoming the basis for our everyday discourse, functional knowledge, social identification, and meaning-making, can we find collaborative rather than polarizing encounters to enhance moral deliberations and heal moral injuries? Much of the moral divide that exists in our culture seems to be driven by the modes of non-collaborative discourse, and sometimes by actual strategic distortion of the views of others, than by a commitment to build bridges and find new alternatives in the interest of the whole. Since much of our personal moral consciousness is built by our current cyber culture, how we find ways to negotiate this system of moral enculturation and meaning-making is a curious question and a compelling moral challenge that remains at the end of the day.

Finally, these questions of collaborative engagement of contending moral positions in church and culture are not abstractions. There are many places they emerge as soul-wounding moral challenges in church and ministry, as well as in politics and culture. I found that the discourse on race and on sexual identity and sexual orientation to be particularly difficult in my workshops with the Endorsed Community of the United Methodist Church. Holding a collaborative frame to encounter these painful disagreements was extremely difficult. One of the most compelling questions with which I am left at the of the day is, How can American Christianity as a whole take charge of its moral dissonance and dilemmas about race and sexual orientation in ways that prevent or minimize moral injury through its means of discourse? A corollary question follows: How can American Christianity structure its life so that those morally injured by its discourse and practices about race and sexual orientation find solace, hope, and healing?

Habits of Mind Exercise: Concluding Inner Dialogue

The final habits of mind exercise invites you to begin with your inner dialogue about the author's reflections in the Conclusion. What was curious, exciting, and challenging to you? Then, ask the three questions posed above in the Conclusion: What do you know better now than you did before? How did this book confirm or deepen existing knowledge? Second, what did you discover, learn, or come to understand that you did not know before? Why is this significant to you? How will you act on it? Third, what curious and difficult questions remain for you? What steps will you take to address them? Finally, if you were to have a collaborative conversation with the author, what questions or statements would start the conversation?

For Further Reading

Manjoo, Farhad. "How the Internet Is Loosening Our Grip on the Truth." *New York Times*, November 3, 2016. www.nytimes.com/2016/11/03/technology /how-the-internet-is-loosening-our-grip-on-the-truth.html?rref=collection %2Fcolumn%2Fstate-of-the-art&action=click&contentCollection=tech nology&region=stream&module=stream_unit&version=latest&content Placement=8&pgtype=collection.

Thompson, Deanna A. *The Virtual Body of Christ in a Suffering World*. Nashville: Abingdon, 2016.

Notes

Preface

1. Joshua Greene, *Moral Tribes: Emotion, Reason, and the Gap between Us and Them* (London: Atlantic Books, 2015), Kindle edition: 44.

1. Setting Our Course

1. The story of "Jesus and the Rich Young Ruler" can be found in Mark 10:17-31; Matthew 19:16-29; and Luke 18:18-30.

2. Don DeLillo, "Sine, Tangent, Cosine," *The New Yorker*, February 22, 2016, www.newyorker.com/magazine/2016/02/22/sine-cosine-tangent.

2. Doing the Right Thing

1. Larry Kent Graham, "Healing, Beauty, and Justice: Colors from the Caregiver's Palette" (retirement address, Iliff School of Theology, November 7, 2015).

2. Cf. Larry Kent Graham, *Care of Persons, Care of Worlds: A Psychosystems Approach to Pastoral Care and Counseling* (Nashville: Abingdon, 1992); Graham, *Discovering Images of God: Narratives of Care with Lesbians and Gays* (Louisville: Westminster John Knox, 1997); Graham, "Pastoral Theology as Public Theology in Relation to the Clinic," *Journal of Pastoral Theology* 9 (2000): 1–17; Graham, "Just Between Us: Some Big Thoughts on Pastoral Theology," *Journal of Pastoral Theology* 25, no. 3 (2016): 172–87.

3. Seward Hiltner, *Preface to Pastoral Theology* (New York: Abingdon, 1958).

4. Carroll A. Watkins-Ali, *Survival and Liberation: Pastoral Theology in African American Context* (St. Louis: Chalice, 1999). Jason Whitehead, "Imagining in Pastoral Theology" (unpublished manuscript, 2005).

5. Don S. Browning's groundbreaking book *The Moral Context of Pastoral Care* (Philadelphia: Westminster, 1976) challenged the narrow definition of moral concern and broke open the field of pastoral theology to a richer discourse about pastoral theology as a moral and ethical discipline.

6. Nancy J. Ramsay, *Pastoral Care and Counseling: Redefining the Paradigms* (Nashville: Abingdon, 2004).

7. Cf. Carrie Doehring, *The Practice of Pastoral Care: A Postmodern Approach*, rev. and exp. ed. (Louisville: Westminster John Knox, 2015); Nancy J. Ramsay, "Intersectionality: A Model for Addressing the Complexity of Oppression and Privilege," *Journal of Pastoral Psychology* 63, no. 4 (2014): 453–69.

8. The term *anxious solicitude* is John Patton and Brian Childs's astute definition of care. It wisely understands care as the complex management, on the part of the care provider, of the dissonance between uncertainty about outcomes and commitment to providing solace and guidance to the careseeker in the face of this uncertainty. See John Patton and Brian H. Childs, *Christian Marriage and Family: Caring for Our Generations* (Nashville: Abingdon, 1988).

9. Mary Martin, private communication with author, February 8, 2017.

3. I Am as We Are

1. Karl Barth, *Church Dogmatics*, III/4, trans. G. T. Thomson (Edinburgh: T and T Clark, 1961), 248.

2. For seminal statements, see Gustavo Gutiérrez, *Essential Writings* (Philadelphia: 1996); John B. Cobb and David Ray Griffin, *Process Theology: An Introductory Exposition* (Louisville: Westminster, 1999); Sallie McFague, *The Body of God: An Ecological Theology* (Minneapolis: Fortress, 1993).

3. Quoted in Anne Kiome Gatobu, *Female Identity Formation and Response to Intimate Violence: A Case Study of Domestic Violence in Kenya* (Eugene, OR: Pickwick, 2013), 42. The original quote can be found in John Mbiti, *Introduction to African Religion* (New York: Praeger, 1975), 108.

4. Clara Sue Kidwell, Homer Noley, and George E. Tinker, *A Native American Theology* (Maryknoll, NY: Orbis Books, 2001).

5. Gatobu, *Female Identity Formation*, 41.

6. Ibid., 42.

7. See pages 148–50.

8. Tinker, *A Native American Theology,* 51.

9. George E. Tinker, "An American Indian Theological Response to Ecojustice," in *Defending Mother Earth: Native American Perspectives on Environmental Justice,* ed. Jace Weaver (Maryknoll, NY: Orbis Books, 1996), 160.

10. One way of theorizing the multiplicity and diversity in suffering is through the concept of "intersectionality." Rather than being identified by one dominant factor, intersectionality posits that social groups and individual identities are made up of multiple factors such as race, gender, sexual orientation, religion, nationality, and class. Establishing solidarity across issues and recognizing their interconnections reflects the "I am as we are" orientation I am proposing. See Ramsay, "Intersectionality."

11. Seiji Osawa, Haruki Murakami, and Jay Rubin, *Absolutely on Music: Conversations* (New York: Knopf, 2016).

12. Tapiwa N. Mucherera, *Meet Me at the Palaver: Narrative Pastoral Counseling in Postcolonial Contexts* (Eugene, OR: Cascade Books, 2009), ix.

13. Ibid., 111.

14. Ibid., 110–23.

4. Anchor Points

1. William Ernest Henley, "Invictus," in *The Oxford Book of English Verse, 1250–1900,* ed. Quiller-Couch, Arthur Thomas (Oxford: Clarendon Press, 1902), 1019.

2. Martin Luther King Jr., "I Have a Dream...," speech delivered at the March on Washington, 1963, www.archives.gov/files/press/exhibits/dream-speech.pdf.

3. Adrienne Rich succinctly summarizes the human capacity to transcend painful histories in her poem "Sources: XV." She says that we are all more than "merely the sum of the damages done to [us]." In *Your Native Land, Your Life* (New York: Norton, 1986), 17.

4. I develop the concept of contextual creativity at length in my book, *Care of Persons, Care of Worlds: A Psychosystems Approach to Pastoral Care and Counseling* (Nashville: Abingdon, 1992).

5. The term "habits of mind" as I use it refers to a committed intentionality to self-regulate one's thoughts and responses and to develop disciplined practices for engaging oneself and one's world with openness and strength. I first encountered the term in the resiliency literature. I develop it my own way in this volume. See Andrew Zolli and Ann Marie Healy, *Resilience: Why Things Bounce Back* (New York: Free Press, 2012).

6. Steven Pinker cites research indicating that when there is moral conflict between persons, we tend to misperceive our own motives as well as the motives of others. We consistently put a more charitable view on our own behaviors and a less charitable view on the behaviors of others. Finding a way to greater accountability for our moral actions is hard work! See Steven Pinker, *The Better Angels of Our Nature: Why Violence Has Declined* (New York: Viking, 2011), 491.

7. I use many pastoral vignettes and examples throughout the book. In all cases the identities of the parties and identifying factual details are disguised and pseudonyms used. In some cases, the examples are composites based on actual situations. In other cases, like Pastor Lawson's, they were read and approved before appearing in the book.

8. On the narrative and collaborative theory of constructing knowledge and creating reality, see Harlene Anderson, "The Heart and Spirit of Collaborative Therapy: The Philosophical Stance—'A Way of Being' in Relationship and Conversation," in *Collaborative Therapy: Relationships and Conversations that Make a Difference*, ed. Harlene Anderson and Diane Gehart (New York: Routledge, 2007), 43–62.

9. This vignette is taken from Andrew Schulman, *Waking the Spirit: A Musician's Journey Healing Body, Mind, and Soul* (New York: Picador, 2016), 82–84.

10. Ibid., 83.

11. Ibid., 84.

Introduction to Part II

1. Michael Yandell, an Army veteran who served in Iraq, reports the loss of his moral compass as a result of his war experience. See "The War Within," *Christian Century*, January 7, 2015, 12–13.

5. God as Moral Conundrum

1. Graham, *Discovering Images of God*, 12. In recent years, the field of Christian social ethics has not separated the personal from the public, in which love was understood as the norm of personal and interpersonal matters and justice was understood as pertaining to social change and prophetic engagement. In current thinking and practice, "just love" is a unified ethic, linking the private and the public. See Marvin Mahan Ellison, *Making Love Just: Sexual Ethics for Perplexing Times* (Minneapolis: Fortress, 2012). See also Margaret A. Farley, *Just Love: A Framework for Christian Sexual Ethics* (New York: Continuum, 2006).

2. Graham, *Discovering Images of God*, 175.

3. I am indebted to my friend and colleague, Carrie Doehring, for her metaphorical use of the image of "minding the gap" in theological discourse.

4. The notion of God as embodied is not new, though it sometimes clashes with the spiritual-material dualism of our culture. For a prescient view of the universe as "God's body," see Sallie McFague, *The Body of God: An Ecological Theology* (Minneapolis: Fortress, 1993).

5. Amy Erickson, "God as Enemy in Job's Speeches" (PhD diss., Princeton Theological Seminary, January 2009). Walter Brueggemann, "Some Aspects of Theodicy in Old Testament Faith," *Perspectives in Religious Studies* 26 (1999): 253–69.

6. Brueggemann, "Some Aspects of Theodicy in Old Testament Faith."

7. The following details are a composite from various similar pastoral situations about God's relation to tragic loss. Identities and situations are disguised, but the spiritual and theological dimensions presented here reflect the actual experiences of careseekers.

8. Research on how suffering persons view God's benevolence in the face of their suffering has significant consequences for how they recover from loss. Those ascribing benevolence to God, like Mrs. Burkett, do better than those who do not, like Mr. Burkett. See, for example, Joshua A. Wilt, et al., "Theological Beliefs about Suffering and Interactions with the Divine," *Psychology of Religion and Spirituality* (2016): 1–11.

6. Dissonance and Dilemmas

1. Jonathan Haidt, *The Righteous Mind: Why Good People Are Divided by Politics and Religion* (New York: Pantheon Books, 2012), 270.

2. Ibid., 313.

3. Ibid., chaps. 2–3.

4. Jesse Graham and Jonathan Haidt, "Beyond Beliefs: Religions Bind Individuals into Moral Communities," *Personality and Social Psychology Review* 14 (2010): 140.

5. The discussion that follows is based primarily on Haidt, *The Righteous Mind*, ch. 12.

6. Ibid., 313.

7. For example, in some workshops I conducted on moral dissonance and moral health with United Methodist specialized ministers over a fifteen-month period in

2014–2016, the hardest discussions we had were about the polarization in the United Methodist Church about the inclusion of gays and lesbians and marriage equality. Parties on all sides of this conversation were angry, fatigued, and convinced that any further discussion, including so-called "collaborative conversations," were not only futile, they inflicted further harm. It was a sobering and instructive experience for me.

8. Haidt, *The Righteous Mind*, 312.

9. Gregory Bateson was famous for identifying schizmogenesis as an inevitable or natural property of social systems. For a helpful discussion of schizmogenesis, see Lynn Hoffman, *Foundations of Family Therapy: A Conceptual Framework for Systems Change* (New York: Basic Books, 1981), 40–41, 43–45.

10. Jamie Beachy, "Spiritual Care as Creative Interruption: Exploring a Generative Metaphor for Intercultural Healthcare Chaplaincy" (PhD diss., Iliff School of Theology and University of Denver, 2015), 110–16. Beachy's references to "the face" and to "visibility" are based upon her appropriation of the work of Emmanuel Levinas. Her references to interruption and creativity are from Gordon Kaufman. See Emmanuel Levinas, *Totality and Infinity: An Essay on Exteriority*, trans. A. Lingis (Pittsburgh: Duquesne University Press, 1969); and Gordon D. Kaufman, *In the Beginning... Creativity* (Minneapolis: Augsburg Fortress, 2004).

11. Beachy, "Spiritual Care as Creative Interruption," 112.

12. Ibid.

13. I learned this process through the work of Professor James Loder of Princeton Theological Seminary. I have used and adapted it over the years.

7. Moral Injuries and Wounded Souls

1. After writing my approach to moral healing, I found my way to Brett Litz, et al., *Adaptive Disclosure: A New Treatment for Military Trauma, Loss, and Moral Injury* (New York: Guilford, 2016). They astutely recognize that there are three types of war trauma that have to be treated differently, even though there may be overlapping symptoms. They are life-threat, loss, and moral injury. Their clinical focus is on loss and moral injury in military contexts. I highly recommend *Adaptive Disclosure* for use in specialized therapeutic and pastoral counseling treatment contexts.

2. Roger D. Fallot, "Trauma-Informed Care: A Values-Based Context for Psychosocial Empowerment," in *Preventing Violence Against Women and Children* (Washington, DC: National Academies Press, 2011), 97–116.

3. Private communication with the author, June 6, 2015. Ramsay has led workshops and is writing on rituals as a source of healing grief and loss in caring for the morally injured.

4. The notion of "remaining" comes from Shelly Rambo's brilliant analysis of the spiritual dimensions of trauma. She is one of the many authors who has informed much of what follows in my description of moral injury. See Shelly Rambo, *Spirit and Trauma: A Theology of Remaining* (Louisville: Westminster John Knox, 2010).

5. Pauline Boss, *Loss, Trauma, and Resilience* (New York: Norton, 2006).

6. Nancy J. Ramsay, private communication with the author, June 6, 2015.

7. Chapter 10 offers resources for addressing communal accountability for corporate moral injury.

8. Ta-Nehisi Coates, *Between the World and Me* (New York: Spiegel and Grau, 2015).

8. Healing the Wounded Soul

1. I first heard this distinction from Seward Hiltner, my doctoral mentor.

2. The discussion of the incest survivors recovery group above is a good example of the need to not blame the victim for their injury, but also to strengthen the victim's agency in their commitment to recover from the assault and its resulting moral injury.

3. See Mucherera, *Meet Me at the Palaver*, ch. 3.

4. The reader should not confuse "prehension" with sympathy, empathy, or compassion. It is a palpable immediacy lying prior to sympathy, empathy, and compassion, while also contributing to their emergence. In the total gestalt I am talking about, sympathy, empathy, and compassion may be evident but they are not to be read as synonymous or equal to prehensions. For an illuminating discussion of the limits of empathy and the value of compassion in moral actions, see Paul Bloom, *Against Empathy: The Case for Rational Compassion* (New York: Ecco, 2017).

5. David's story is recounted in Fay A. Marks, "Stories of Nonviolence: Lifting Soul Clouding; The Peace Circle," The Swanlight Organization, February 13, 2004, http://www.swanlight.org/PC_SNVLifting.htm.

6. Ibid.

7. In my work with family responses to war, I discovered two forms of forgiveness. One is proactive forgiveness, which is the forgiveness offered to the offender without any action or request on the offender's part. Like in the case of Chethlahe,

it is self-release. The second is responsive forgiveness, which is the forgiveness that becomes possible in response to the offender taking steps toward remorse, accountability, or restitution. It is the basis for reconciliation and relational healing. Both are separable yet related forms of forgiveness, with strengths and limitations as applied to each situation. See Larry Kent Graham, "Narratives of Families, Faith, and Nation: Insights from Research," *Journal of Pastoral Theology* 21, no. 2 (2011): 1–18.

8. A classic investigation on forgiveness and the Nazi Holocaust can be found in Simon Wiesenthal, Vanessa Hall-Bennett, Harry J. Cargas, Bonny V. Fetterman, and Moline Public Library (Ill.), *The Sunflower: On the Possibilities and Limits of Forgiveness* (Moline, IL: Moline Public Library, 2009).

9. Space does not permit a fuller discussion of forgiveness. For fuller analysis, see Joretta L. Marshall, *How Can I Forgive?: A Study in Forgiveness* (Nashville: Abingdon, 2005); Larry Kent Graham, "Exploring Forgiveness of Veteran Guilt through Collaborative Pastoral Conversation," *Sacred Spaces* 5 (2013): 146–71.

9. Healing Collaborations

1. See the Habits of Mind Exercise: The Hypnagogic Soul–Collaborative Conversation with Myself in chapter 6 for details about this exercise.

2. John Patton, *Is Human Forgiveness Possible?: A Pastoral Care Perspective* (Nashville: Abingdon, 1985). Patton astutely recognizes that rage is a defense against shame.

3. For example, sometimes when I got stuck writing my book, and willpower failed me, I asked for my imagination to speak to me in the night. Frequently, I found some new thoughts coming into my head. I became a receptor rather than agent. Sometimes daydreaming got me there too.

4. See the Habits of Mind Exercise: The Hypnagogic Soul–Collaborative Conversation with Myself in chapter 6. Substitute a similar story or put this one in your own words.

5. Litz et al., *Adaptive Disclosure*, 126–39.

6. I adapt these positions from family therapy to moral processes. See David Kantor and William Lehr, *Inside the Family: Toward a Theory of Family Process* (Cambridge, MA: Meredith Winter Press, 2003).

7. Carrie Doehring, "Resilience as the Relational Capacity to Integrate Moral Stress," *Journal of Pastoral Psychology* 64 (2015): 635–49.

8. See how revising moral orientations was a factor in Mr. Burkett's moral injury (chapter 5) and in the incest recovery group (chapter 7).

9. For more detailed examples of veteran healing from moral injury, see Larry Kent Graham, "Exploring Forgiveness of Veteran Guilt." See also David Lee Jones, "The Ambiguity of War," *The Living Pulpit*, October–December 2005, 25–27. David Jones describes a moving encounter with his World War II veteran father in which healing of moral injury becomes possible.

10. Healing Rituals and Memorials

1. Harold S. Kushner, "Seder of Safe Return: For the Families of American Jews Who Served Our Country in the Cause of Freedom 2003–5763," Neshama: Association of Jewish Chaplains, accessed May 17, 2017, www.najc.org/pdf/Seder_of_Safe _Return.pdf.

2. Soul Repair Center, "Pathways to Hope for Moral Injury and Other Invisible Wounds: A Service of Welcome, Remembrance, and Hope," October 28, 2015, www.brite.edu/wp-content/uploads/2013/07/October-28-2015-Service-bulletin -.pdf.

3. The material of this chapter is built upon but goes beyond some of my previous lectures and writings on public pastoral responses to disaster community trauma. See Larry Kent Graham, "Political Dimensions of Pastoral Care in Community Disaster Response," *Journal of Pastoral Psychology* 63, no. 4 (2014): 471–88; and Larry Kent Graham, "Pastoral Theology and Catastrophic Disaster," *Journal of Pastoral Theology* 16, no. 2 (Fall 2006): 1–17.

4. Edwin Muir, "The Wheel," in *Collected Poems* (New York: Oxford University Press, 1960), 105. Cited in Donald W. Shriver, *An Ethic for Enemies: Forgiveness in Politics* (New York: Oxford University Press, 1995), 12.

5. Kathleen M. O'Connor, *Lamentations and the Tears of the World* (Maryknoll, NY: Orbis Books, 2002), 3, 96.

6. Ibid., 102.

7. Kathleen D. Billman and Daniel L. Migliore, *Rachel's Cry: Prayer of Lament and Rebirth of Hope* (Cleveland: United Church Press, 1999), 104.

8. For an overview of the role of religious communities and their leaders in each phase of corporate responses to communal disruption, see Graham, "Political Dimensions of Pastoral Care."

9. A fuller account and discussion of this interview can be found in Larry Kent Graham, "Narratives of Families, Faith, and Nation: Insights from Research," *Journal of Pastoral Theology* 21, no. 2 (2011): 1–18.

10. Nijaz Alispahic, "Nadrastanje Boli [Overgrowth of Pain]" in *Karakazan*. Radio Kameleon Tuzla, Bosanska Biblioteka Klagenfurt/Celovec-Austria, Lojze Weiser: 1996. Translated text "Overcoming Pain," as printed here, was communicated to the author in an interview with the translator, who prefers to remain anonymous. Used by permission of author and translator.

11. See "14th Anniversary Tuzla Massacre 25.05.2009 (pictures)," YouTube, posted by "cupotz," May 30, 2009, www.youtube.com/watch?v=pC0dZVezaDk.

12. I learned afterward that the commander who ordered the shelling was tried for crimes against humanity in the Hague and given a twenty-five year prison sentence. In some respects, their prayer for the offenders to be punished was realized, at least in part.

13. Storm Swain, *Trauma and Transformation at Ground Zero: A Pastoral Theology* (Minneapolis: Fortress, 2011).

14. James 1:2-4.

15. The Soul Repair Center at Brite Divinity School has led the way in addressing veteran moral injury. See their website at www.brite.edu/programs/soul-repair/.

16. Assessing causations for complex social disruptions is complex. I have found the work on resiliency by Zolli and Healy to be especially useful to examine causes of things falling apart (*Resilience: Why Things Bounce Back* [New York: Free Press, 2012]).

17. Lisa Gough, ed., *Never Forget: The Story Behind the Vietnam Veterans Memorial* (Washington, DC: Vietnam Veterans Memorial Fund, 2008), 20.

18. Ibid., 87–103.

19. Ibid., 88.

20. See Kim Phuc, "Address at the United States Vietnam War Memorial," November 11, 1996, http://gos.sbc.edu/p/phuc.html; and Kathryn Hawkins, "Child of War Turned Peace Activist: Phan Thi Kim Phuc," Gimundo, January 31, 2008, http://gimundo.com/news/article/child-of-war-turned-peace-activist-phan-thi-kim-phuc/.

21. This paragraph is based upon an extensive investigative report by Ronald N. Timberlake. See "The Fraud Behind the Girl in the Photo: Hijacking the History of the Vietnam Veteran," Vietnam Memoirs, January 1999, www.ndqsa.com/myth.html.

22. See "Pastor Admits Lying about Vietnam Bombing," 11th Armored Cavalry's Veterans of Vietnam and Cambodia, January 12, 1998, http://www.11thcavnam.com/education/pastor_admits_lying_about_vietna.htm.

23. Museums of memory are growing institutions helping to preserve the memory of the past, interrogate causes, struggle with contending narratives, and assess accountability. See, for example, the Holocaust Museum (Washington, DC), Museum of Memory and Human Rights (Chile), and Tuol Sleng Museum of the Crimes of Genocide (Cambodia).

24. See the 9/11 Memorial and Museum website at www.911memorial.org/mission.

25. Elizabeth Hernandez, "Gov. Hickenlooper Apologizes to Descendants of Sand Creek Massacre," *Denver Post*, December 3, 2014, www.denverpost.com/news/ci_27060084/gov-hickenlooper-apologizes-descendants-sand-creek-massacre.

26. The United Methodist Church as a whole is lamenting its history of genocide and colonization of Native Americans in the United States and Canada. Alongside their local preparation in Colorado, the Rocky Mountain Conference participated in the denomination-wide study of the United Methodist Church's relationship to all indigenous people over two centuries of their intermingled lives.

27. These words are from a University of Denver website report on its study of DU's relationship to the Sand Creek massacre. See www.du.edu/explore/history/sand-creek.html.

28. Rebecca S. Chopp, "Higher Education and Democracy: Imagining a New Relationship" (chancellor's inaugural address, University of Denver, September 18, 2015), http://inauguration.du.edu/wp-content/uploads/2015/09/chancellors-address-transcript.pdf.

29. George E. Tinker, "GC2012: George Tinker, Act of Repentance," YouTube, posted by General Conference United Methodist Church, April 27, 2012, www.youtube.com/watch?v=v-DoOCp5XA0&feature=youtu.be.

30. See Graham, "Political Dimensions of Pastoral Care," 486.

References

9/11 Memorial and Museum. www.911memorial.org/mission.

11th Armored Cavalry's Veterans of Vietnam and Cambodia, "Pastor Admits Lying about Vietnam Bombing." January 12, 1998. http://www.11thcavnam.com/education/pastor_admits_lying_about_vietna.htm.

"14th Anniversary Tuzla Massacre 25.05.2009 (pictures)," YouTube, posted by "cupotz," May 30, 2009, www.youtube.com/watch?v=pC0dZVezaDk

Anderson, Harlene. "The Heart and Spirit of Collaborative Therapy: The Philosophical Stance—'A Way of Being' in Relationship and Conversation." In *Collaborative Therapy: Relationships and Conversations that Make a Difference*, ed. Harlene Anderson and Diane Gehart, 43–62. New York: Routledge, 2007.

Barth, Karl. *Church Dogmatics*, III/4. Translated by G. T. Thomson. Edinburgh: T and T Clark, 1961.

Beachy, Jamie. "Spiritual Care as Creative Interruption: Exploring a Generative Metaphor for Intercultural Healthcare Chaplaincy." PhD diss., Iliff School of Theology and University of Denver, 2015.

Billman, Kathleen D., and Daniel L. Migliore. *Rachel's Cry: Prayer of Lament and Rebirth of Hope*. Cleveland: United Church Press, 1999.

Bloom, Paul. *Against Empathy: The Case for Rational Compassion*. New York: Ecco, 2017.

References

Boss, Pauline. *Loss, Trauma, and Resilience*. New York: Norton, 2006.

Brock, Rita Nakashima, and Gabriella Lettini. *Soul Repair: Recovering from Moral Injury after War*. Boston: Beacon, 2012.

Browning, Don S. *The Moral Context of Pastoral Care*. Philadelphia: Westminster, 1976.

Brueggemann, Walter. "Some Aspects of Theodicy in Old Testament Faith." *Perspectives in Religious Studies* 26 (1999): 253–69.

Chopp, Rebecca S. "Higher Education and Democracy: Imagining a New Relationship." Chancellor's Inaugural Address, University of Denver, September 18, 2015, http://inauguration.du.edu/wp-content/uploads/2015/09/chancellors-address-transcript.pdf.

Coates, Ta-Nehisi. *Between the World and Me*. New York: Spiegel and Grau, 2015.

Cobb, John B., and David Ray Griffin. *Process Theology: An Introductory Exposition*. Louisville: Westminster, 1999.

Doehring, Carrie. *The Practice of Pastoral Care: A Postmodern Approach*. Rev. and exp. ed. Louisville: Westminster John Knox, 2015.

————. "Resilience as the Relational Capacity to Integrate Moral Stress." *Journal of Pastoral Psychology* 64 (2015): 635–49.

Ellison, Marvin Mahan. *Making Love Just: Sexual Ethics for Perplexing Times*. Minneapolis: Fortress, 2012.

Erickson, Amy. "God as Enemy in Job's Speeches." PhD diss., Princeton Theological Seminary, 2009.

Fallot, Roger D. "Trauma-Informed Care: A Values-Based Context for Psychosocial Empowerment." In *Preventing Violence Against Women and Children*, 97–116. Washington, DC: National Academies Press, 2011.

Farley, Margaret A. *Just Love: A Framework for Christian Sexual Ethics*. New York: Continuum, 2006.

References

Gatobu, Anne Kiome. *Female Identity Formation and Response to Intimate Violence: A Case Study of Domestic Violence in Kenya*. Eugene, OR: Pickwick, 2013.

Gough, Lisa, ed. *Never Forget: The Story Behind the Vietnam Veterans Memorial*. Washington, DC: Vietnam Veterans Memorial Fund, 2008.

Graham, Jesse, and Jonathan Haidt. "Beyond Beliefs: Religions Bind Individuals into Moral Communities." *Personality and Social Psychology Review* 14 (2010): 140–50.

Graham, Larry Kent. *Care of Persons, Care of Worlds: A Psychosystems Approach to Pastoral Care and Counseling*. Nashville: Abingdon, 1992.

_____. *Discovering Images of God: Narratives of Care with Lesbians and Gays*. Louisville: Westminster John Knox, 1997.

_____. "Exploring Forgiveness of Veteran Guilt through Collaborative Pastoral Conversation." *Sacred Spaces* 5 (2013): 146–71.

_____. "Healing, Beauty, and Justice: Colors from the Caregiver's Palette." Retirement Address, Iliff School of Theology, November 7, 2015. https://docs.google.com/document/d/107dRO0puXTsz1kaQxmczMjq3uCA0nYhUqO Vi2CPlqN8/edit.

_____. "Narratives of Families, Faith, and Nation: Insights from Research." *Journal of Pastoral Theology* 21, no. 2 (2011): 1–18.

_____. "Pastoral Theology and Catastrophic Disaster." *Journal of Pastoral Theology* 16, no. 2 (Fall 2006): 1–17.

_____. "Political Dimensions of Pastoral Care in Community Disaster Response." *Journal of Pastoral Psychology* 63, no. 4 (2014): 471–88.

Greene, Joshua. *Moral Tribes: Emotion, Reason, and the Gap between Us and Them*. London: Atlantic Books, 2015.

Gutiérrez, Gustavo. *Essential Writings*. Philadelphia: Fortress, 1996.

References

Haidt, Jonathan. *The Righteous Mind: Why Good People Are Divided by Politics and Religion.* New York: Pantheon Books, 2012.

Hawkins, Kathryn. "Child of War Turned Peace Activist: Phan Thi Kim Phuc." *Gimundo,* January 31, 2008. http://gimundo.com/news/article/child-of -war-turned-peace-activist-phan-thi-kim-phuc/.

Henley, William Ernest. "Invictus." *The Oxford Book of English Verse, 1250–1900.* Edited by Arthur Thomas Quiller-Couch, 1019. Oxford: Clarendon Press, 1902.

Hernandez, Elizabeth. "Gov. Hickenlooper Apologizes to Descendants of Sand Creek Massacre." *Denver Post,* December 3, 2014. www.denverpost.com/news /ci_27060084/gov-hickenlooper-apologizes-descendants-sand-creek -massacre.

Hiltner, Seward. *Preface to Pastoral Theology.* New York: Abingdon, 1958.

Hoffman, Lynn. *Foundations of Family Therapy: A Conceptual Framework for Systems Change.* New York: Basic Books, 1981.

Jones, David Lee. "The Ambiguity of War." *The Living Pulpit* (October–December 2005): 25–27.

Kantor, David, and William Lehr. *Inside the Family: Toward a Theory of Family Process.* Cambridge: Meredith Winter Press, 2003.

Kaufman, Gordon D. *In the Beginning... Creativity.* Minneapolis: Augsburg Fortress, 2004.

Kidwell, Clara Sue, Homer Noley, and George E. Tinker. *A Native American Theology.* Maryknoll, NY: Orbis Books, 2001.

Kushner, Harold. "Seder of Safe Return: For the Families of American Jews Who Served Our Country in the Cause of Freedom 2003–5763." *Neshama: Association of Jewish Chaplains.* www.najc.org/pdf/Seder_of_Safe_Return.pdf.

LaDuke, Winona. *All Our Relations: Native Struggles for Land and Life.* Cambridge, MA: South End, 1999.

References

Lebowitz, Shana. "A Stanford Professor Explains How 'Design Thinking' Can Help You Lose Weight, Stop Worrying, and Change Your Life." *Business Insider*, February 1, 2016. www.businessinsider.com/stanford-professor -design-thinking-achieve-your-goals-2016-2.

Levinas, Emmanuel. *Totality and Infinity: An Essay on Exteriority*. Translated by A. Lingis. Pittsburgh: Duquesne University Press, 1969.

Litz, Brett T., Leslie Lebowitz, Matt J. Gray, and William P. Nash. *Adaptive Disclosure: A New Treatment for Military Trauma, Loss, and Moral Injury*. New York: Guilford, 2016.

McFague, Sallie. *The Body of God: An Ecological Theology*. Minneapolis: Fortress, 1993.

Marks, Fay A. "Stories of Nonviolence: Lifting Soul Clouding; The Peace Circle." The Swanlight Organization. February 13, 2004. http://www.swanlight.org /PC_SNVLifting.htm.

Marshall, Joretta L. *How Can I Forgive?: A Study in Forgiveness*. Nashville: Abingdon, 2005.

Mbiti, John. *Introduction to African Religion*. New York: Praeger, 1975.

Mucherera, Tapiwa N. *Meet Me at the Palaver: Narrative Pastoral Counseling in Post-colonial Contexts*. Eugene, OR: Cascade Books, 2009.

Muir, Edwin. "The Wheel." In *Collected Poems*, 105. New York: Oxford University Press, 1960. Cited in Donald W. Shriver. *An Ethic for Enemies: Forgiveness in Politics*, 12. New York: Oxford University Press, 1995.

O'Connor, Kathleen M. *Lamentations and the Tears of the World*. Maryknoll, NY: Orbis Books, 2002.

Ozawa, Seiji, Haruki Murakami, and Jay Rubin. *Absolutely on Music: Conversations*. New York: Knopf, 2016.

Patton, John. *Is Human Forgiveness Possible?: A Pastoral Care Perspective*. Nashville: Abingdon, 1985.

References

Patton, John, and Brian H. Childs. *Christian Marriage and Family: Caring for Our Generations*. Nashville: Abingdon, 1988.

Phuc, Kim. "Address at the United States Vietnam War Memorial." November 11, 1996. http://gos.sbc.edu/p/phuc.html.

Pinker, Steven. *The Better Angels of Our Nature: Why Violence Has Declined*. New York: Viking, 2011.

Rambo, Shelly. *Spirit and Trauma: A Theology of Remaining*. Louisville: Westminster John Knox, 2010.

Ramsay, Nancy J. "Intersectionality: A Model for Addressing the Complexity of Oppression and Privilege." *Journal of Pastoral Psychology* 63, no. 4 (2014): 453–69.

————. *Pastoral Care and Counseling: Redefining the Paradigms*. Nashville: Abingdon, 2004.

Rich, Adrienne. "Sources: XV." In *In Your Native Land, Your Life*, 17. New York: Norton, 1986.

"Sand Creek." University of Denver. www.du.edu/explore/history/sand-creek.html.

Schulman, Andrew. *Waking the Spirit: A Musician's Journey Healing Body, Mind, and Soul*. New York: Picador, 2016.

Shaw, Tamsin. "The Psychologists Take Power." *New York Review of Books* 63, no. 3 (February 25, 2016): 38–41.

Shriver, Donald W. *An Ethic for Enemies: Forgiveness in Politics*. New York: Oxford University Press, 1995.

Soul Repair Center. "Pathways to Hope for Moral Injury and Other Invisible Wounds: A Service of Welcome, Remembrance, and Hope." October 28, 2015. www.brite.edu/wp-content/uploads/2013/07/October-28-2015 -Service-bulletin-.pdf.

Swain, Storm. *Trauma and Transformation at Ground Zero: A Pastoral Theology*. Minneapolis: Fortress, 2011.

References

Tick, Edward. *War and the Soul: Healing Our Nation's Veterans from Post-Traumatic Stress Disorder*. Wheaton, IL: Quest Books, 2005.

Timberlake, Ronald N. "The Fraud Behind the Girl in the Photo." Vietnam Memoirs. January 1999. www.ndqsa.com/myth.html.

Tinker, George E. "An American Indian Theological Response to Ecojustice." In *Defending Mother Earth: Native American Perspectives on Environmental Justice*, ed. Jace Weaver, 153–76. Maryknoll, NY: Orbis Books, 1996.

————. "GC2012: George Tinker, Act of Repentance," General Conference United Methodist Church, April 27, 2012. https://www.youtube.com /watch?v=v-DoOCp5XA0&feature=youtu.be.

————. "A Theological Introduction to Cross-Cultural Issues." In *Creation and Culture: The Challenge of Indigenous Spirituality and Culture to Western Creation Thought*, 1–7. New York: Lutheran World Ministries, 1987.

Watkins-Ali, Carroll A. *Survival and Liberation: Pastoral Theology in African American Context*. St. Louis: Chalice, 1999.

Whitehead, Jason. "Imagining in Pastoral Theology." Unpublished manuscript, 2005.

Wiesenthal, Simon, Vanessa Hall-Bennett, Harry J. Cargas, Bonny V. Fetterman, and Moline Public Library (Ill.). *The Sunflower: On the Possibilities and Limits of Forgiveness*. Moline, IL: Moline Public Library, 2009.

Wilt, Joshua A., Julie J. Exline, Matthew J. Lindberg, Crystal L. Park, and Kenneth I. Pargament. "Theological Beliefs about Suffering and Interactions with the Divine." *Psychology of Religion and Spirituality* (2016): 1–11.

Yandell, Michael. "The War Within." *Christian Century* (January 7, 2015): 12–13.

Zolli, Andrew, and Ann Marie Healy. *Resilience: Why Things Bounce Back*. New York: Free Press, 2012.

CPSIA information can be obtained
at www.ICGtesting.com
Printed in the USA
LVOW08s1928030617
536790LV00006BD/7/P